The Not Forgotten War:

One Soldier's Story

Nicholas Dick Jr.

AN [*e-reads*] BOOK
New York, NY

Copyright 2002 by Nicholas Dick Jr.
First e-reads publication 2003
www.e-reads.com
ISBN 0-7592-5766-3

As told to Janet Dailey

Table of Contents

Prologue

OUTPOST HARRY

KOREA, JUNE 11, 1953

It was close to midnight and everything was as black as hell. I was hunkered against the wall of the trench, waiting like everyone else, but not sure what was coming. Something told me if there was ever a hell on earth, it was right there on Outpost Harry.

The floor of the trench was slimy with blood — and God knows what else — from last night's fighting. The air reeked with the stench of death, most of it coming from the corpses of the Chinese, piled like sandbags alongside the trench near the foot of Harry, all killed during the previous night's assault on the outpost.

The big question was — would the Chinese make another attempt to take the outpost? They had damned near overrun it the night before, but our guys managed to throw them back after some savage hand-to-hand fighting in the pitch darkness.

Sitting there in that inky black night, seeing the sheen of the bayonet I had fixed to my rifle, waiting and wondering if there would be a repeat of the Chinese assault, I was about as scared as a twenty-year old can be.

Nobody was doing much talking. It was quiet. Too quiet. And too dark. I had been in Korea for less than a month, but that was long enough to learn that the Chinese preferred to launch their assaults in the dead of night. And that's just about what time it was.

My nerves were stretched tighter than a tenor string. Part of me kept hoping that the Chinese had learned their lesson the night before, but the Chinese never seemed to care how many of their men got

1

killed as long as they got their objective. And Outpost Harry was their objective.

Suddenly the silence was shattered by the eerie blare of a bugle coming from the blackness beyond the trench. At almost the same instant, a green flare arced across the night sky, and the air screamed with the distinctive whine of incoming artillery rounds.

Before the ground shook with the first explosion, I had a glimpse of hunched-over figures, bathed in the weird green glow of the dying flare, as they flooded out of the trees on the opposite slope in a human wave. It was a sight straight out of a nightmare, except it was real.

Those bastards were attacking!

For a split second, I wondered what in hell was I doing there. How in the world had I gotten myself into this situation.

One

My journey began the usual way — with that letter every young guy dreaded receiving back during the Korean War. 1952 was the year they drafted twenty-year olds. Sure enough, on my twentieth birthday, November 1, 1952, there was that infamous "Greetings" letter in the mailbox, informing me that "my friends and neighbors" had selected me, Nicholas Dick, for service. Some birthday present.

To be honest, I wasn't exactly thrilled about being drafted. I knew they were still fighting over there in Korea, even though it wasn't front-page headlines anymore. Mostly any stories about the Korean conflict dealt with peace talks and were usually buried somewhere in the back pages.

Korea wasn't like World War II where an American soldier fought for his country. Korea was considered a police action, much like Bosnia today; you were fighting for someone else's country.

And anybody who was gung-ho to get involved in the conflict had already enlisted. Trying to dodge the draft wasn't something people talked about back in the Fifties. That came later, during the Vietnam War. The idea of avoiding the draft certainly never crossed my mind, not when I had two older brothers who had served during World War II, John in the Marines and Irwin in the Navy.

But, I promise you, during those intervening three weeks before I had to report, I partied like hell.

Then, on November 20 1952, I showed up at the Council Bluffs Water Works Building, as ordered. From there, myself and the other draftees were loaded on a bus and driven across the Missouri River to Fort Omaha, where they gave us our physicals.

Looking back, I can't help but wonder whether things might have turned out differently if I had better understood my rights back then.

I have since been told that I should have received a medical deferment because I had one leg shorter than the other and a hole in my right eardrum. Who's to say? I guess that's water you can't pick up and put on the other side of the bridge.

Right or wrong, the doctors that day said I had passed my physical. I was in the Army. To make it official, the other inductees and I were told to stand, raise our right hands and be sworn in. The Army guy addressing us also stated that anyone who failed to do so would be subject to immediate arrest.

Believe me, a threat like that will scare any twenty-year old kid into raising his right hand, whether he wants to or not.

And at twenty years old, you're still a kid, although I didn't think I was at the time. But I was definitely a kid.

After the swearing-in ceremony, they took us to dinner at some fancy place near Fort Omaha. It was kinda like the condemned being treated to a hearty meal.

When we finished eating, they took us back to Fort Omaha and loaded us onto a bus. Off we went to Camp Crowder, Missouri, just outside of the small town of Neosho, south of Joplin. There was no going home to tell your folks you were leaving, no last goodbye to friends or loved ones, no nothing. You were in the Army, and that was that.

Camp Crowder is where I was issued my Army uniforms — and where I sent my civilian clothes back home. It's also where I learned how to march and salute and all those good military things.

I don't remember anymore exactly how long we were at Camp Crowder. Everything moved so fast then, with new things being thrown at me all the time. I knew I was on the move, that I was going somewhere, but I never really had time to think about what was happening to me. I figure the Army probably planned it that way.

Anyhow, one day they loaded us onto another bus. South on Highway 71, we went, all the way to Camp Polk, Louisiana, somewhere southwest of Alexandria. Back then, Camp Polk — today it's called Fort Polk — was the Ohio National Guard place, so I wore a little red dot on the shoulder of my uniform as a patch.

After we arrived at our barracks, they lined us up and assigned us to our sergeant. He proceeded to tell us the do's and don'ts, will's and wont's of the Army and what we would be expected to do.

Like I said before, I was only twenty years old. All of it was new to me, and a little scary, too. I remember standing in line wondering what I was going to do. A lot of other guys, I discovered later, felt the same way.

One officer talked to us and said, essentially, "If you want to get out of the Army fast, be a good boy for two years and you're out. If you're a bad boy, I promise you that you will be here a lot longer than two years."

That definitely made me want to be a good boy, because I didn't want to be in the Army one day longer than my two- year hitch.

It was at Camp Polk where I went through my basic training. That was quite an experience for me, but so were my surroundings. Back home in Iowa, it was the dead of winter. But in Louisiana, it was warm; at least it seemed warm to a boy who'd never been down south before.

At this point, I guess I should back up a minute and explain that I was born in Illinois. When I was thirteen, my folks picked up and moved to Council Bluffs, Iowa. That was just about the extent of the traveling I'd done. And in case you don't know it, the scenery doesn't change a whole lot between Illinois and Iowa. Or the weather either, for that matter.

Both the weather and the scenery were a whole lot different in northern Louisiana. I remember we would be marching along in the sunlight, when all of a sudden it would rain and hail, then back it went to warm weather again.

On top of that, Camp Polk is located in a swampy area. The ground was so boggy and loose that when a deuce-and-a-half — that's a two-and-a-half ton truck the Army uses for a troop carrier for you non-veterans — would leave the area where our bivouac was, you could actually see the ground wiggle under it.

One of the first things the Army did after we arrived at Camp Polk, was to lecture us new recruits about water moccasins, deadly pencil snakes, scorpions and all the nasty little insects that lived around there. They also gave us a bunch of shots to protect us as much as they could, but sometimes you have to use your own common sense for protection, too.

As for the initial eight weeks of basic training itself, all of it seemed like a game to me at the time. The Army had us running everywhere we went. If you were caught walking, it was on the ground and ten pushups. Then they'd jump it up to twenty, then thirty, then forty. By the end of eight weeks, a guy could do fifty.

It was the same with the high bar they had outside of the mess hall. Every recruit had to do so many chin-ups before he went inside to eat. This was all in addition to the daily calisthenics they had us doing.

The physical part of it was rigorous, that's for sure. And I didn't understand the need for it. This was the modern Army I was in, a mechanized force with Jeeps and tanks and troop carriers. I had no way of knowing that South Korea had few roads, and most of what the Koreans called roads wouldn't qualify even as a good cow path back in Illinois and Iowa, let alone be considered a road.

But I'm getting ahead of myself again.

Naturally during basic, we had a lot of rifle training. We would go out to the firing range and practice shooting at targets. I was pretty good with a rifle, probably because I'd done a lot of hunting while I was growing up back on the farm. As near as I can remember, they never did wave Maggie's drawers over any of my targets.

For those of you who don't know, Maggie's drawers are what the soldiers call the red flag that's waved when a shooter completely misses his target.

In basic, the Army also tried to simulate combat conditions. They would bombard some hill with an artillery barrage, giving the artillery guys a chance to practice while other recruits, like me, would move to the base of the hill and get the feel of the rounds going over our heads and shells exploding. The Army used real ammunition so the noise was loud, the ground shook, and your heart got to pumping at a pretty good rate.

After the artillery quit, we recruits would charge up the hill and take control of it. The Army really tried to make it seem like the real thing, but it felt more like an adult version of some childhood game, with special effects added.

Naturally, we had plenty of lessons in hand-to-hand combat as well. Among other things, we were taught how to pop out the enemy's eyeballs with your two thumbs, and how to deafen him by slapping his ears real hard, how to flip him as well as other judo moves designed to cripple him.

I didn't understand what good it did to cripple the enemy instead of simply killing him? But the sergeant explained that wounding an enemy could be better than killing him, because it took about four of their guys to look after the wounded man and get him off the front-line. That means four guys are taken out of combat. It's the same reasoning behind setting booby traps, especially the kind that maim rather than kill.

We had a lot of practice in the use of bayonets, learning how and where to stab your enemy, and what to do on the off chance the bayonet became stuck in the enemy. Most of the time that wouldn't happen. I don't know if you've ever looked closely at a bayonet before, but it has these grooves along the blade. The grooves create little air pockets that make it easier to pull the bayonet out. Without them, the wound would create a vacuum and hold onto the blade.

If the blade became lodged in his backbone, the grooves weren't effective. If that happened, we were told to make sure th
ere was a round in the gun, so you could pull the trigger and blow the guy off of your bayonet.

Another thing the Army made us do — both in hand-to-hand fighting and bayonet practice — that made absolutely no sense to me. That was having to yell AAAHHH! every time you stabbed the practice dummy. If you forgot to yell like that, you had to do it again.

It seemed so stupid to me that I finally asked the sergeant, "Why do we have to yell this Aaahh shit? It's silly."

That sergeant didn't even blink. "Have you noticed that every time you yell like that, your brain doesn't function? You aren't thinking to yourself — I'm going to stab this guy here or there. You aren't even thinking about killing him. In fact, you aren't thinking at all about what you're doing; you're simply doing it. By the time you finish your training, this will become so deeply ingrained in you that when you find yourself in a combat situation, your training will take over. And when you see a bunch of enemy soldiers coming at you, firing, you'll start yelling and open fire. You won't think — I'm killing these guys. Maybe when it's over, you will, but not at that precise moment."

What he said made sense. But, at the time, it also sounded like a lot of bullshit, too, if you'll pardon my language.

While we were on maneuvers, myself and some other guys in my unit were assigned to protect our headquarters. We saw two GIs come into our camp. No big deal.

Pretty soon they walked out of the command post with our company commander. Once they were outside of the perimeter where we are, they said, "Do you realize that we just captured your command because not a single one of you challenged us when we walked up?"

I thought they had pulled a lousy trick. These guys were GIs. Why should we challenge them? But it was also pretty danged embarrassing. It's the kind of lesson a guy doesn't forget, though. I certainly didn't.

One of those crazy coincidences that makes the world seem really small, happened to me during basic. I had been at Camp Polk for only a couple weeks when I noticed a guy across the way who looked very familiar. Then it hit me. It was Bernard Kinnaman, my sister Myrtle's brother-in-law from Nebraska.

Kinnaman had actually received his draft notice before I got mine. But he needed some sort of operation, so the Army gave him a deferment until after he had recovered from the operation. In the meantime, I was drafted and sent to Camp Polk. Now Kinnaman had showed up at the same place.

As it turned out, this wasn't the only time I would run into Kinnaman unexpectedly.

Anyhow, basic training normally lasts for eight weeks if you're in a rifle company. But I had been dropped off at D Company, which is a heavy weapons company. I didn't know the difference until I reached the end of my eight weeks, and the Army informed me that I would now go into my special training.

"What special training?" I said.

That's when I found out that I was in heavy weapons, which meant I had another eight weeks of training to go, making for a total of sixteen weeks.

Back in the early Fifties, heavy weapons consisted of .30 caliber water-cooled machine gun, .30 caliber air-cooled machine gun, .50 caliber air-cooled machine gun, 0.2 mortar, .81 millimeter mortar, 4.2 mortar and .75 recoilless rifle.

I probably should explain that, in the Army, a battalion is made up of four companies — three rifle companies and one heavy weapons company. The machine gunners in the heavy weapons company get divided up and assigned to a rifle company. Technically speaking, you're still in D — or Dog — Company, but, for instance, you're attached to A Company. I know it's confusing, but that's the Army's way of doing things. Surprise.

There are advantages to being in heavy weapons. Two of the biggest are that you don't have to man listening posts or go out on patrols. Those jobs belong to the soldiers in the rifle companies. Also, when you're in heavy weapons, you do most of your traveling from place to place in a Jeep while the rifle companies slog it out on foot.

During those last eight weeks, I was trained in the operations and usage of various weapons. I can sum most of it up this way — you know all those war movies you've seen where a guy swivels a machine gun from side to side to spray a wide target area or where he picks up the machine gun and fires it from the hip like it was a submachine gun? That's all a lot of Hollywood baloney.

If you want to spread a bunch of rounds over a wide arc, you don't swing the whole machine gun; you simply tap the side of the barrel. And as for picking up a machine gun and firing it like an automatic rifle, forget it. A guy would need the strength of Atlas to keep the barrel level. If he tried it, more than likely he would wipe out half of his own outfit.

Plus, you fire a machine gun in short bursts. There is none of that prolonged shooting like you see in the movies. In the first place, the gun would probably overheat and lock up on you. More importantly, it's a waste of ammunition. And in combat, there isn't an endless supply of ammunition to waste.

Sometime, during that final two weeks of the sixteen-week training, we were sent out on bivouac for a week or two. While we were out there, they asked for volunteers to go back to camp and clean up before everybody returned. I was quick to volunteer, thinking that one day at camp was better than one day out on bivouac, especially since I had some booze stashed in our barracks.

Back then, I was somewhat of a heavy drinker — at least, by today's standards. But that's what you did in the Fifties for fun; you and your buddies would grab some beer and get drunk. We didn't have the drugs around that the kids face today.

Anyhow, all of us volunteers were taken back to our barracks. We cleaned up the place, had a couple drinks, and waited to be taken back to the bivouac area. Only nobody came. Somehow or other they forgot we were the barracks. As long as the booze held out, we weren't exactly eager to bring it to anybody's attention.

Finally, on the last day of bivouac, the sergeant walked in, stared at us and said, "What the hell are you guys still doing here?"

"Nobody came back to get us."

He swore a little, then said, "Come on. We have to get you out to the firing range." (I should explain here that this is where we had to crawl on our bellies while they fired a machine gun over us, using live ammunition.) "If you guys don't do that," the sergeant said, "you won't graduate."

So he loaded us in his Jeep and raced off to the firing range. I'm glad to say all of us finished the course — and also had five days of loafing and drinking.

Then our orders came down. Out of our entire group, there was one guy who was being sent to the U.S. base in Guantanamo Bay, Cuba. All the rest of us were bound for Korea.

Ignorance is a wonderful thing. Maybe that's why young people have so much of it. While I wasn't what you would call happy about being sent to Korea, I don't recall being all that scared at the idea. A little worried, maybe, and uncertain about what it might be like. But I wasn't scared, not like one guy I heard about, who ended up going AWOL rather than go to Korea.

I guess when you're young, you're certain you are going to live forever. And in all those war movies, John Wayne never got seriously hurt. It was always the other guys.

On my last day at Camp Polk, I went to see my sergeant When I went to his room, he invited me in and said, "How about a beer?"

"What?" I stared at him like he'd gone loco. Here was the sergeant asking me to have a drink with him.

He looked at me and smiled a little. "You're not a recruit anymore, Nick. You're a soldier." He handed me a bottle of beer. "Just remember what we put you through, and you've got it made."

We talked for a little bit and drank the beer. Then he said, "Go on. Get your buddies and have some fun. And good luck in Korea."

It turned out that I needed every bit of that luck he wished me, and then some.

Shortly after I talked to the Sarge. I called my folks to let them know that I was coming home on a ten-day leave and that I had received orders sending me to Korea.

10

While I was on the phone with my mom, she told me about a friend of mine, named Warren Krogan, who was in the Air Force. Before he joined up, Warren had been in an auto accident and hurt his knee. The injury had bothered him a little, but not that much.

Then one of the Air Force doctors took a look at it and discovered that Warren had bone cancer. My mom told me that Warren was going to have his leg amputated.

The news came from out of the blue. Warren was like a brother to me — and he was going to lose his leg. His leg! I started crying.

The other guys saw me and thought I was crying because I was getting sent to Korea. When I got off the phone, they started razzing me about it. I hauled off and decked one of them. I know I shouldn't have, but it stopped the laughing. Thankfully I settled down after that.

Now that I had my orders and my ten-day leave, I was in a rush to get home. So I flew out of Alexandria, Louisiana, to Omaha.

The weekend after I arrived home, my folks, my brother Irvin and I drove to Henry, Illinois to visit my oldest brother John. One afternoon while we were there, the three of us boys were sitting around talking. Naturally the subject came around to my pending departure to Korea. When it came to combat, both of my brothers could speak with experience. As a Marine, John had seen action in the Pacific Theater during World War II, and as a Navy man, Irvin had been on the Atlantic side.

John remarked, "If the Chinese and North Koreans fight anything like the Japs did, you are in for a rude awakening."

At the time, I didn't really understand what he was talking about. And, fresh from sixteen weeks of training, I was pretty confident of my ability. You might say, cocky.

Later in the conversation, my brother Irvin said, "If you get killed in Korea, Nick, I'll join up to avenge your death."

I looked at him and said, with all the confidence in the world, "You don't need to worry about doing that. There is no North Korean or Chinese who is man enough to kill me."

After we got back from Illinois, I spent the days with my folks, and the nights with my buddies, partying like hell.

My orders called for me to ship out of Tacoma, Washington. So, after being home seven days, I boarded a train for Tacoma. I was in no hurry to get there, not like when I flew home. I don't remember much about the train ride, but I'd wager I spent most the trip in the club car, sipping beer.

What can I say? When I work, I work hard. And when I play, I play hard. And I planned on having a good time right up to the minute when I boarded that ship bound for Korea.

Two

When I arrived in Tacoma, Washington, my ship was waiting for me. The USNS. Marine Adder. I can't tell you exactly what type of ship it was. A troop carrier of some sort, but on the small side as Naval ships go. I know they jammed us in there, bunk stacked on top of bunk.

It's ironic, but out of all the guys who were in basic training with me, all with orders shipping them to Korea, not one of them was aboard the Marine Adder. Out of our training class, I was the only one there.

Anyhow, I was told it would take us approximately two weeks to get to Japan by ship. After we were at sea about a week, early one morning we ran into a heavy storm, complete with gale-force winds.

To be honest, I thought I would take to the sea. After all, sailing should be in my blood. My grandfather Pieter Dick was a sea captain who sailed out of Denmark back during the days of the old windjammers. Four times he went around the world.

My dad was always telling me about the times when, as a boy, he used to sneak on board his father's ship. He would ring the ship's bell, then hide underneath a canvas. Everybody would come out, wanting to know who rang the bell. After they left, he would ring it again and hide.

Just about everybody in the Dick family were sailors, except for my father and me. Actually my dad sailed, too, until he lost his hearing. Shortly after that happened, he decided to come to America where he eventually married my mother. His uncle urged him to come back to Denmark.

But my dad said, "I'm an American. If I wanted to live in Denmark, I would have stayed there."

While I was growing up, my dad rarely spoke Danish, and he absolutely refused to teach the language to any of us kids. He wanted us to be Americans.

When he wanted to, my dad could be real bullheaded.

Back during World War II, my dad's half-brother Johannes Christian Dick served in the Danish Navy. He went through World War II and the German occupation-of Denmark. Then, about a year after the war ended, he was on a ship that struck a loose mine. He was killed.

It always seemed like such a waste to me that he had been killed well after all the fighting was over. Such a horrible waste.

It was something that stuck with me while I was in Korea.

Anyhow, I was on Marine Adder in the middle of this storm. They had everything buckled down and allowed no one to go outside on deck. The ship was doing about two knots an hour, just enough to maintain steerage while trying to ride out the storm.

And it was one wild ride, with the ship climbing up to the crest of a tall wave, then diving down it with the stern momentarily lifting out of the water and the props churning air. Each time that happened, the ship vibrated so violently that I thought for sure we were on our way to the bottom.

Now, I have a good strong stomach, but all that rolling and rocking made me just a tad bit queasy. I remembered my brother Irvin, who had been in the Navy, had told me that if I started getting seasick, I should eat. So I went up to the mess hall, galley or whatever they call it on a ship, and started eating.

Not far from me, there was a bunch of guys throwing up all over the table. I turned my back on them and kept eating, but I started feeling really queasy. Once I got the food down, I decided to go back and lie down on my bunk for awhile. So I headed for the ladder. There I was on the bottom rung when this guy threw up all over my shoes. That was it. I lost it.

Believe me, I was one sick puppy until the worst of the storm finally blew over and they let us out on deck. The fresh, briny smell of that sea air was great, but I still remember how the waves rolled and slapped against the bow. They were still higher than our ship. Imagine how much taller they must have been when the storm was the most severe.

Standing out on that deck made me think about my seafaring grandfather and wonder what it must have been like riding out a rough storm on one of those windjammers.

Sometime after the storm was over, we crossed the International dateline. All of us were presented with a certificate to mark the occasion. I ended up sending mine home to my mom.

At the end of approximately two weeks at sea, we arrived in Japan. I have to admit, it always seemed weird to me that I sailed west in order to reach the Far East command.

Anyhow, we sailed into port. There I was standing on deck, watching all the Japanese on shore waving to us. Just ten years earlier, they were the enemy we had hated so much. Now they were waving a welcome to us. It was a very odd feeling.

From the ship, we were taken to a military base that had previously been Japanese. I still remember that the bunks in the barracks were made out of real thin wood; they were nothing at all like regular Army bunks.

A few years earlier that same barrack had been filled with Japanese soldiers; now it was occupied by a bunch of Americans. It was only 1953; World War II hadn't been over that long.

We slept in the barracks that night. The next morning, they checked our shot records. Somewhere along the line there had been a royal snafu. The record for my inoculations had gotten lost, which meant I had to have my shots all over again — all fourteen of them. The doctors wanted to split the shots and spread them over a couple of days.

But I said, "No. Give all of them to me at one time."

So they did.

It so happened that on that very same day, we were issued our weapons for combat in Korea. The next morning we were supposed to go out on the range and test-fire them. But after all the shots that I'd received the day before, I couldn't lift either my right arm or my left. I needed help just getting dressed. Luckily the sergeant took my weapon and test-fired it for me.

A day later, we were loaded onto another ship, bound for Korea this time. On board the ship, I met a skinny kid named Bob from Ohio. Maybe he wasn't quite as skinny as I remember, but I've always had a husky build so most people look slender to me.

For some reason the two of us hit it off right away.

Maybe because both of us came from similar backgrounds where neither of our families had a lot of money to spare for anything that wasn't absolutely essential. That was one of the reasons Bob was so happy about being in the Army.

You see, prior to his service, he had very bad teeth because his parents couldn't afford for him to see a dentist. But once he was in the Army, they pulled them all and gave him a set of dentures. For the first time in his life, Bob had good teeth. He was really proud of that. That was something a lot of other guys couldn't understand, but I did.

When we reached the waters off of Inch'on our ship weighed anchor to wait for high tide. At low tide, Inch'on Harbor is all mud flats, making it virtually impossible for any vessel to enter. But at high tide the water in the harbor is only about thirty feet deep, making the difference between high and low tide one of the most extreme in the world. It's also what made MacArthur's invasion at Inch'on, back in 1950 such a touch-and-go thing.

Once the tide started coming in, we went down a set of steps on the outside of the ship and climbed into an amphibious landing craft.

The ride to shore was something else. There was the city of Inch'on in front of us. Most of the buildings along the waterfront were still pock-marked from the bombardment that had preceded the MacArthur's invasion. Off to the right, a small cargo ship was tied up to the dock. On the other side of the harbor, I noticed a bunch of small Korean fishing boats, sitting high and dry on the mud flats.

Farther inland from the boats, fishing nets were strung up to dry. I noticed some Koreans hanging something on the nets, but I couldn't tell what it was. I asked one of the other guys if he knew.

"I'm not sure, he said. "But they might be drying fish."

Later on I found out he was right. Dried fish, as well as rice, is one of the staples of the Korean diet.

As our landing craft drew closer to shore, I saw more damage from the shelling back in 1950. It hit me that, coming in like this, on a barge with a bunch of other soldiers, it was like all those war movies I'd seen. Only this wasn't make-believe; this was real.

I know this probably sounds a bit corny, but it was kind of cool and exciting.

Bob must have felt the same way, because he leaned over and said to me, "This is neat, isn't it? Makes you feel kinda like John Wayne, doesn't it?"

"Yeah." I was embarrassed to admit it, but it was true. It felt exactly like something out of a John Wayne movie. "I don't think we'd better tell anybody else, though. They wouldn't understand."

"You're probably right." He nodded to the troop trucks parked near our landing point. "I wonder where we'll go when we board those deuce-and-a-halfs waiting for us."

The sergeant happened to be standing close by and overheard his comment. "You'll all be taken to the REPL depot."

"What the heck is a REPL depot?" I asked. That was a new acronym I hadn't heard before.

"It's a replacement and rotation point. That's where they'll feed you, give you your papers, tell you where you're going and what your new outfit will be."

"Sounds good," Bob said, then turned to me, "Where do you think you'll be sent?"

"I'm not sure. They trained me in heavy weapons, but I don't know if they'll keep me there. How about you?"

"I only had eight weeks of basic, so I'll probably get stuck in the infantry."

Just as the sergeant said, after we landed, they loaded us onto the deuce-and-a-halfs and took us to the REPL depot. That night I slept in a bunker, lined with sandbags.

Those sandbags had a smell to them that I'll never forget — an odor that was something greenish and musty. It reminded me of an old root cellar, one of those earthen caves the farmers used to dig to store their fruits and vegetables in over the winter months.

The odor probably came from some chemical they used to treat the sandbags. That night I was certain it would make me sick if I had to smell it very long. Like most things though, I eventually got used to it.

When they called us out the following morning, May 17, 1953, I was informed of my status and asked if I wanted to go into mortars, the .75 recoilless rifle, or machine guns.

A part of me still had images of John Wayne in my brain. I said to Bob, "I'm going to take machine guns. My brother John was a machine gunner in the Marines."

Bob replied, "Well, I don't have any choice. I'm heading to a rifle company."

Now it was official. I had been assigned to the Third Infantry Division, Fifteenth Regiment. In the Army, the Fifteenth was known as the "Can Do" regiment, because if something needs to be done, they "can do" it. It was also Audie Murphy's regiment during World War II.

Since Bob was headed for a rifle company, he climbed into one deuce-and-a-half and I boarded a different one. From the REPL depot, the truck traveled inland, away from the muddy flatness of the western coast. I had my first good glimpse of the Korean countryside.

The terrain quickly changed to a series of broad sweeping valleys and hills, studded with scrubby brush. Just about everywhere you looked, there were rice paddies, sometimes with white-clad farmers working in them.

It was late spring. The forsythia and wild plums had finished their blooming, but the hills and valleys were shaded in rich greens, which made the white of the rice workers clothes stand out in contrast. The exposed soil was reddish-brown in color, nothing at all like the black dirt back home in Iowa and Illinois.

That ride also gave me my first good whiff of the countryside. Growing up on a farm, I was very familiar with the smell of manure, whether from a cow, pig or sheep. But this smell was different, stronger and extremely rank.

It turned out that the Korean farmers used human waste to fertilize their rice fields, turning the rice paddies into virtual cess ponds.

Driving through a village, it was common to see a farmer dumping a chamber pot into the back of his horse-drawn wagon, then moving on to empty the chamber pot left outside the next house. As he rolled along, liquid excrement dripped out of the back of his wagon onto the road behind him. "Honey wagons" is what they were called, probably because of the flies that swarmed around them wherever they went.

Truthfully, the countryside was beautiful — as long as you didn't breathe in.

My destination turned out to be the Iron Triangle area where the Fifteenth Regiment was stationed along the Main Line of Resistance, better known by its Army acronym MLR.

At that time, I had no idea what the Iron Triangle was, let alone where it was. I was told it was along the 38th parallel, but you couldn't have proved it by me.

Later I found out that it was technically north of the famous 38th parallel. The term Iron Triangle was originally used to describe a vital supply and communication area with the towns of Hwach'on, Ch'orwon, and Kumwha at its points. All three were linked by rails, that formed the shape of a crude triangle.

After the U. N. Forces captured the southern point of Hwach'on, the media correspondents liked the phrase Iron Triangle so much that they created a new one by inverting the triangle shape, placing the town of Plyongyang, instead of Hwacho'on, as its northern point and leaving the towns of Ch'orwon and Kumwha as its base.

When we reached the MLR the deuce-and-a-half pulled up behind a hill and stopped. I was told this is the end of the line for me and that someone would be along to pick me up. I grabbed my gear and climbed out of the truck to wait by the road.

Farther up the hill, I spotted a half-track with a quad .50 mounted on it. And the quad .50 was blazing away. I knew it was mostly used as an antiaircraft weapon, so I gave the sky a scan, but I couldn't see anything.

Not far from my position, there were some .81 mortars, but they were quiet. Still, the shooting made it clear I was in the front line area.

I sat and waited while the other guys who had ridden with me were met and taken away to their new positions. I hadn't sat there very long when a soldier came walking over the bank of a hill straight toward me. He was on the short side, slender-built, with glasses.

He walked up to me. "Are you Private Dick?"

"I am."

"I'm Blackburn. I'm here to take you to our machine gun position. Are you ready?"

"Sure." I gathered up my gear and followed after him when he headed back the way he'd come.

All the while the quad .50s continued to fire. Blackburn didn't pay much attention to them, but I was curious — and a little nervous, too.

"What's all the shooting about?" I asked. "They're firing on Jackson Heights. Last night, some Chinese were spotted in no-man's land over in the vicinity-of Outpost Harry. The Chinese have a route that goes up over Jackson Heights to their position behind it. That's the route the quad .50s have targeted."

There I was in Korea, fresh out of basic training, in a place where there had been enemy activity the night before. This did not sound good to me.

"Outpost Harry, is that where we're going?" I asked, feeling uneasy and trying not to show it.

"No. We're on the MLR behind Outpost Tom. In this sector, there are a trio of outposts," Bradburn explained. "They're called Tom, Dick and Harry. I'd guess there's probably a couple miles between each outpost. Tom sits on that hill ahead of us; Dick is located off to our right in the valley; and Outpost Harry is beyond that, on top of another hill. Tom and Harry command the approach routes to Seoul and the rest of southern Korea. The Eighth Army has classified all three as major outposts and has issued standing orders that they're to be held at all costs."

This definitely did not sound good to me.

I was still trying to figure out how I felt about this when the road completed its curve around the hill where the quad .50 sat.

A big broad valley stretched away from the road. The entire area was blanketed with a patchwork of green rice paddies.

Blackburn pointed to the sweep of land and said, "That's the Ch'orwon Valley."

He made the name sound important, but it was meaningless to me, as well as hard to pronounce.

"What's the Ch'orwon Valley?" I asked.

"It's one of the richest valleys in Korea where most of the rice used to be grown. It runs, more or less, north to south. All those paddies are lying dormant, gone to seed. No one's allowed to work in them anymore. It's too hard to tell the enemies and friendlies apart. That's no man's land now."

About this time, I heard a whistling sound over my head. Maybe I was green, but I knew an artillery round when I heard one. After everything Blackburn had told me about current enemy activity in the area, I heard that sound and immediately ducked.

Not Blackburn. He just looked back at me as calm as you please and said, "That's out-going mail. The artillery is firing on Jackson Heights."

"How can you be so sure it's ours?"

"Once you've been here awhile, you'll be able to tell the difference between rounds coming in and those going out. In the meantime, don't worry. I'll let you know when it's incoming mail."

"Thanks. I appreciate that. I'd just as soon not get blown to hell my first day here." I tried to make a joke of it, but there was a part of me that was dead serious.

"I'll try to help as much as I can, Nick," Blackburn promised with a grin. "I've only been over here a two or three weeks myself, though."

He wasn't what you would call an old-timer, but it was obvious to me that he knew more than I did.

Three

Once we were around the hill, Blackburn and I left the road and began walking along the top of an old dike that had been built for the rice paddies in the valley.

"That is what we call no man's land," Blackburn told me as he pointed north. "Nobody is ever supposed to be out there. If you see anyone, you're supposed to shoot him. That big hill over there, that's Jackson Heights. And over there, are some tanks that the First Cavalry had to abandon back during the early part of the war. You can't see them very well from here without binoculars, but the Chinese have just about stripped them of anything that was of value

As we walked along the dike, I noticed some ammunition that looked as if it had been dumped in the ditch below. I started to ask Blackburn about it when I heard that whistling sound again.

"Duck!" Blackburn yelled at me and threw himself flat onto the ditch. "That's incoming."

I hit the dirt about as fast as he did.

As we lay there, he pushed his glasses back on his nose and grinned at me. "Did you hear the difference? The sound of the one coming in has a steady pitch. When the rounds are going out, they have an uneven spiraling sound."

I couldn't actually say I had noticed, but I would listen for it the next time.

The explosion, when the shell hit, was fortunately nowhere near us. We stood up, dusted ourselves off and started walking again.

"They tell me that if you don't hear it coming, that's the round that will kill you," Blackburn volunteered.

"Do you think that's true?" I wondered.

"I don't know," Blackburn admitted. "But I hope I never find out."
I heartily agreed with that.

I'm not sure how far we walked, but it was a good ways before we finally reached the trenches of MLR. When I say trenches, you have to throw out all those World War II movies with John Wayne and visualize instead the trenches of World War I, that are about six foot deep and three foot wide.

In other words, the trenches are roughly the dimensions of a grave, except that they snake all along the MLR.

Blackburn turned off the main trench onto a side one that led to our machine gun bunker. Unlike the trenches, a bunker is roofed. The height of it is tall enough that a man can stand up in it, but its walls are still dirt. Along the outer wall, facing the valley floor and the approach to the outpost beyond us, there was a raised dirt platform about three foot high. The machine gun was mounted on top of it with its muzzle jutting out of the window-like opening in the wall, padded with sandbags.

Our sleeping quarters occupied a different area of the bunker. Instead of spreading our sleeping bags — fart sacks, we called them — on the hard ground, they had erected makeshift cots out of concertina posts, or steel posts, and commo wire, communication wire. The wire was strung between the posts to make a modern version of an old rope bed. (Which is where we get the expression 'sleep tight'.)

Blackburn pointed to one of the cots. "That's your bunk. The other guy rotated out."

In all, Blackburn explained there were four of us assigned to this particular machine gun bunker. The guy manning the machine gun was Corporal Pendleton from Texas; he was on the good-looking side, maybe an inch or so taller than me and well muscled, definitely not skinny like Blackburn. I don't remember the assistant gunner's name for sure anymore. It might have been Joe. Anyway, it was his job to feed the ammunition into the gun.

Blackburn and I were ammo bearers. It was our responsibility, in this case, to obtain ammunition from the ammo bunker when the supply at our position ran low. The rest of the time, we protected the approach to the bunker with our carbines.

Much of the area beyond the trenches was ringed with barbwire that was strung between concertina posts to slow down any enemy attack on our position. Empty cans of C rations hung at intervals from the wires, obviously to create noise when disturbed and warn of any movement out there.

Every so often they had what they called 'trip flares' that were strung higher than the rest. If anything broke that wire, it would trigger a flare.

In the valley to the left of the machine gun position, I could see the ruins of a town, long abandoned. Railroad tracks still led in and out of it, indicating it must have been of importance at some time or other.

Slightly to the right, there was a road of sorts that led to a hill sitting all by itself in the valley. On that hill was Outpost Tom.

After I stowed my combat gear, Blackburn filled me in about life in a frontline bunker. For food, we had the Army's famous C rations. On the MLR, a soldier didn't have the luxury of a mess tent where he could go to have his meals. The Army did provide one hot meal a day to the troops on the MLR, but that meal was served at three o' clock in the morning. Which left C rations for the rest of our meals.

So Blackburn showed me the way food was heated on the frontline. He took four .30 caliber shells, removed the lead, powder and primer out of them, then placed them under a shelf that had been dug into the side of the trench about two foot off the ground. Then he took some C-3 explosives and placed a little piece of it under the shelf, opened a can of C rations, set it on top of the shelf, and lit the C-3. It burned instantly and warmed the contents of the can.

This method didn't get the food what you would call hot; it was more like lukewarm.

I remember one time we had a new replacement join us and ask how to heat his food. We told him to take a handful of C-3 explosive, put it under the shelf and put his can of C rations on top of it, unopened, then light the C-3. He did.

That can blew up, just like we knew it would, and covered him from head to toe with beans and wieners. We laughed like crazy, but he didn't think it was one bit funny.

Blackburn also clued me in on the enemy's tactics and their penchant for attacking at night. Daytime was when you got all the rest you could; the onset of darkness brought the greatest threat from the enemy. Nighttime was when they preferred to strike.

In other words, just about everything bad happened at night in Korea. Maybe that's why I still have so much trouble at night.

Ask any veteran or historian who has studied the Korean War and they will tell you that the Chinese were very shrewd and clever. They recognized early that the strengths of the American Army were centered on its planes, tanks and artillery. So they searched out its weaknesses, such as a lack of training in night-fighting and hand-to-hand combat, the fear of its soldiers over being cut off from the rear, and the inability of its planes to provide air support at night.

These weaknesses they exploited, and avoided, whenever possible, encounters in open country where the mechanized might of the American Army could be brought to bear. Unfortunately or fortunately, depending on your viewpoint, Korea's rough and broken terrain, as well as its lack of an adequate road system, suited the guerilla-like tactics of the Chinese perfectly.

My first couple nights at the bunker were quiet ones. But on the evening of May 21, 1953, that changed. Two patrols were sent out, one with a war dog and its handler. Somewhere around midnight, we heard shooting and caught glimpses of muzzle flashes some distance away on the valley floor.

I knew one of those patrols was catching hell. No one had to tell me to stay awake. I was wide awake, and every unit was placed on one hundred per cent alert.

On and off all night long, there were scattered firefights in the area we called no man's land. Some were brief, and some lasted longer. At different times, our artillery, tanks and mortars opened fire. And the Chinese artillery replied with barrages of their own.

The exploding shells sounded just as loud as the ones I heard in basic training. And the ground tremors felt just as strong. While physically the barrage felt the same, my mental reaction to it was very different. I knew that, unlike in basic training, those in-coming rounds wanted to take somebody out, — and I was among those somebodies.

Along about dawn when the light was all gray and muted, we were notified that one of the patrols would be returning through our sector, and that we were to provide supporting fire, if needed. I was at my post guarding the machine gun bunker, watching for the patrol to show.

All that night, the wind had blown. But with the approach of sunrise there wasn't the faintest breath of a breeze to be felt anywhere.

Someone told me that Korea is known as "land of the morning calm". That morning there was utter stillness. Nothing moved except misty fingers of fog creeping up the hillside. The air was laden with the lingering smell of powder smoke, an odor that's been embedded in my mind ever since.

At last the patrol emerged from that smoky fog and began making their way through the barbed wire to the trenches. The sight of those soldiers is one I'll never forget. Their feet were dragging, and the exhaustion on their faces was like nothing I had ever seen before. That, and the blank, half-dead look in their eyes.

A couple of them were wounded and being helped along by their buddies. Then I spotted one of the soldiers carrying the dog. I knew right away the dog was dead.

During the night I had suspected that the fighting out there in no man's land was bad. But the absolute fatigue in their faces and the way they seemed to drag themselves told me more loudly than words that they had just come through hell.

These were guys just like me. This wasn't some Hollywood combat movie. This was the real thing. This was war. And it shook me good.

It's probably one of those things where you had to be there and see their faces for yourself to understand why it affected me the way it did. But the scene haunted me all day long. It still does.

The following afternoon, a soldier came walking up the side trench to our machine gun bunker, saw me and said, "Nick. Hey, man, it's good to see you."

You can imagine how surprised and happy I was when I finally recognized Bob from Ohio, the guy I'd met on the boat from Japan. It was almost as good as seeing a familiar face from back home.

"How in the world did you know I was here?" I asked.

"I saw you up here yesterday morning when my patrol came in. Even with a helmet on, that mug of yours is pretty easy to recognize, Nick."

"You were on that patrol?" I had stared at the tired and drawn-out faces of those men pretty hard. I was surprised that I hadn't noticed Bob being among them. "I don't remember seeing you."

"I was there."

"It looked like you guys had a bad time of it." But I was still wondering how I had missed recognizing him.

"It was rough, Nick. Real rough." When he said that, — just for a minute — I had a glimpse of that look I had seen in the eyes of those men. Then he glanced away and it was gone. "We got into a firefight with some Chinese. Then, later we ambushed one of their patrols."

I could tell he didn't want to talk about what he'd been through. It was something I didn't understand until later.

"How did the dog get killed?" That seemed the safest question. "Did the Chinese get him?"

"No. The dog started barking, and his handler didn't have any choice but to kill him before he gave our position away. War dogs are trained to be silent, but this one — something went wrong, and he barked."

We talked awhile longer. Then Bob had to leave and get back to his outfit. He said he would drop by and see me again.

That was one of the advantages of being assigned to a machine gun bunker; your buddies always knew where they could find you.

After a couple more days on the MLR, we were rotated back to the Wyoming Line — back in blocking, we called it. There we finally got a shower, some clean clothes and a hot meal at the mess tent, not to mention a re-supply of cigarettes and some beer, Korean-made.

And we had mail call, but no letters had caught up with me yet.

I felt a little awkward sitting around, just killing time while the others read their mail from home. Blackburn must have noticed.

"Here, Nick." He offered me a couple of his letters. "It will be awhile before any of your mail catches up with you. Why don't you read some of mine until it does."

"No, thanks. Those are your letters."

But Blackburn insisted. "I don't mind if you read these. Go ahead. Take them."

I didn't really want to read his mail, but the offer to share his personal letters from home was so generous and thoughtful that it seemed an insult to turn him down. It was a gesture I'll never forget. But that was Blackburn, always quick to think about the other guy.

Back in blocking, it wasn't all rest and relaxation. The Army continued to train us to keep us sharp for when we had to go back on line. But all too soon, it was our turn to rotate to the front again.

It was the night when I finally made the trip to Outpost Tom on a personnel carrier; the personnel carrier was like a tank without a top on it. This time, in addition to human cargo, the carrier had a load of building materials for the outpost. Which meant, we ended up sitting on top of some logs.

When that driver left the MLR, he had the pedal to the floor. We went full blast over that trail to Tom to prevent the enemy artillery from zeroing in on us. It was one rough ride, too, bouncing over dikes and ditches and rice paddies. For us passengers, it was a bit like trying to stay on a bucking bronco. I hung on to anything I could grab to keep from being thrown out, because I knew that driver didn't dare stop to pick me up without risking an artillery round taking out everybody out.

Somehow we all made it to the outpost in tact and were assigned to a machine gun position along the left slope.

One of the first things I noticed when we reached the outpost was a jackhammer drilling into some rock on the hill. I asked around to find out what was going on. I was told that a crew from the construction battalion was building a huge bunker, big enough to hold everybody on the outpost. There was to be a steel door installed at the entrance to the bunker. Now I understood why the personnel carrier had been hauling logs.

The plan was — or so I was told — that if the enemy overran the outpost, we would all go inside the bunker and close the door. Supposedly explosives were rigged throughout the trenches. If the enemy ever gained possession of the hill, someone inside the bunker would set off the explosives. Afterwards we were supposed to go out and mop up any of the enemy that might have survived.

Nothing about this plan sounded very reassuring to me. Common sense told me that the Army wouldn't build something like this unless they thought they might need it. And that started me wondering what the Army brass knew that I didn't.

There was some scuttlebutt going around Outpost Tom that there was an increase in Chinese activity and troop movement going on behind the enemy-held Jackson Heights. Sure signs, I was told, of a forth-coming Chinese offensive.

On my second night on Tom, June 2,1953, we were placed on one hundred per cent alert. The listening post, located beyond the barbed wire directly in front of our machine gun bunker, had reported sighting enemy patrols in the area.

There wasn't much doubt we were going to see some action. Two guys in another rifle company were scheduled to rotate back to the States in a couple of days. Rather than take the risk of getting shot or killed when they were so close to going home, they talked to the other guys in their outfit, and all of them agreed that the two guys should find themselves a safe place and stay there.

In the hillside above the trenches, the Chinese had dug deep holes, back when they had held this same ground. The entrances to these holes were small, but once you were inside, the area opened up into a cave-like space. We called them "Chink holes".

Anyway, these two guys climbed up to one of them and took refuge inside.

Not long after the outpost was put on alert, a small firefight broke out around the listening post. The radio immediately started chattering with voices yelling, "We're out'a here. We're coming in. We're coming in. Give us fire."

From my position, I had a clear view of the slope below me. As I watched, the guys who had been manning the listening post wove their way along the designated path through the barbed wire. They looked scared as hell to me, and I figured they probably had good cause.

One of the commanding officers called for the "moonbeam". "Moonbeam" is the name the GIs gave to one of those powerful, World War II era searchlights. It was located on high ground all the way back on the Wyoming line, with its light trained on Outpost Tom.

When that light came on, it illuminated the entire left slope of the hill. Suddenly the whole area was as bright as day.

For the most part, the hillsides on Outpost Tom, below the trench work were steep, except on the left side where I was stationed. There, the slope overlooking the Ch'orwon Valley was gradual, making it the logical choice for any enemy attack.

Even with the moonbeam shining on the slope, I still didn't see anything moving once our guys from the listening post made it safely through the wire to the trenches. But from the base of the hill and beyond, it was all pitch-black. I couldn't see anything, not a rock, a bush, or an enemy soldier. But I knew the Chinese were out there. Somewhere. But where, was the question.

I propped myself against the dirt wall of the trench, breathing in that now-familiar musty smell of earth and sandbags. I had my flak jacket on, my helmet on my head, my carbine loaded and a round in the firing chamber.

Nervously I scanned the slope again. But there still wasn't anything to see. As I stared in the inky blackness, searching for any distinguishable shape, my palms started sweating. I didn't know what was coming, and I was scared. Scared that I wouldn't know what to do and freeze, scared that I'd let my buddies down, — scared of a hundred nameless things.

Unconsciously, I started praying under my breath.

"The Lord is my shepherd. I shall not want. He maketh me to lie down in green pastures; he leadeth me beside the still waters. He restoreth my soul: he leadeth me in the paths of righteousness for his name's sake. Yea, though I walk through the valley of the shadow of death, I will fear no evil: for thou art with me; they rod and thy staff they comfort me. Thou preparest a table before me in the presence of mine enemies; thou anointest my head with oil; my cup runneth over. Surely goodness and mercy shall follow me all the days of my life: and I will dwell in the house of the Lord forever."

I recited the entire Twenty-third Psalm.

I wasn't by any stretch of the imagination the religious kind. It's true that while I was growing up, my parents made sure I attended Sunday School and went to church every week. I was definitely raised to believe in God, but I was never one to read the Bible or even attend church regularly once I became an adult.

But you show me a man who claims he never prayed in war time when he was scared and facing the enemy, and I'll show you a liar.

Me, I prayed. And there isn't any doubt in my mind that the Lord was with me that night — and a lot of other nights in Korea.

Suddenly, in the darkness at the base of the hill, I spotted a small flare of light, the kind made when a cigarette is being lit. It was followed in seconds by the murmur of voices, yakking away in some foreign language that I guessed to be Chinese.

I watched that red pinprick of light and listened intently to the voices. All the while, my nerves were strung so tight they were humming.

An officer came by and saw the way I was focusing on that light, my carbine sighted on a spot just below it.

"Don't concentrate too much on just one object or you'll start seeing one of the damned concertina posts moving," he told me.

I knew that was probably good advice, but that little glow of light and those foreign-murmuring voices told me we had enemy soldiers down there. I was so intent on watching for some movement, some distinguishing shape that would give me a target that I never saw the two Chinese soldiers who were creeping through the barbed wire.

Suddenly one of them rose up and hurled a hand grenade toward our machine gun bunker. It exploded against the slope above me, unleashing a hail of rock and dirt into the trench and onto me. A stone fragment hit me on the mouth and I all but dug a hole in the side of the earthen wall, trying to find cover from it, knocking my helmet off in the process. As gunfire opened up around me, zeroing in on those two Chinese, I grabbed my helmet with a shaky hand and pushed it back on head.

The guy next to me swore in a shocked voice, "Jeezus, I've been hit."

Glancing over, I saw blood on his hand. More streamed from a gash on the back of his neck along an area of exposed skin just below his helmet and above his flak jacket.

I took one look at that wound, minor though it was, and vowed that wasn't going to happen to me. Right there and then I loosened my helmet liner and pushed my steel pot low over my ears, making sure the back of my helmet overlapped the top of my flak jacket.

About the time the wounded guy went off to find a medic, Blackburn came out of the bunker and joined me. By then I was busy checking the slope below us and realizing just how close that grenade had come to landing in the trench where I was. I thanked God that it hadn't and began reciting the Lord's Prayer in earnest, knowing that this fight wasn't over.

"Our Father, who art in Heaven, hallowed be Thy name." At that point, I didn't particularly care if Blackburn or anybody else thought I was a religious nut. That grenade had shaken me up — and made me mad.

Just about then, I saw a Chinese soldier rise up in a crouch and start to run across an open stretch. Without thinking, I opened fire about the same time everybody else on the whole outpost did. The machine gun chattered away from the bunker on my right, tracer bullets flying.

Above the racket I heard the high, steady whines of artillery shells. Blackburn yelled, "Incoming! Incoming!"

I flattened myself against the trench wall and my helmet went flying again. I grabbed for it as the whole hill seemed to shake with a series of deafening explosions. Rock and dirt flew everywhere.

Round after round after round fell on the hill. Just about the time that I thought it might be safe to raise my head, another one landed with a thunderous roar, spewing smoke and dirt everywhere. Again I hugged the ground for dear life. I never felt so helplessness in my whole life.

After what seemed an eternity, the shelling slacked off, leaving the hill cloaked in a haze of dust and greasy smoke. I scrambled to the edge of the trench, certain that the cessation of the barrage signaled the start of an enemy attack.

Sure enough, I caught a glimpse of a couple of Chinese soldiers in mustard-colored caps darting along the shadows near the base of the hill. Gunfire erupted up and down the line, and I joined in with my rifle.

From the darkness came the muzzle flashes of return fire. More grenades exploded, some landing short of our trenches and blowing holes in the barrier wires.

But there was no massed charge like I expected. The Chinese were all spread out across the slope, bent over in a low crouch, creeping forward singly or in twos and threes, somehow managing to blend in with the landscape and moving with a kind of stealth.

We managed to drive them back.

Within minutes, it seemed, the shelling started again. It was a pattern that continued off and on throughout the entire night. There was never time to draw an easy breath, never time to relax. I was on edge every minute, my heart hammering, the adrenaline pumping. Fear was always there, clawing at my throat.

At one point during the shelling, a round exploded so close that the concussion practically lifted me off the ground. Almost simultaneously Blackburn and I were both pelted with hot fragments. Then the ground shook with more blasts. I never had a chance to dwell on any one explosion. They were all blurred together.

I lost track of time. In my mind, the mix of fighting and enemy artillery bombardment took place over a two-hour time span, three at the most. After we had repulsed the last attack, I noticed the eastern sky lightening with the gray of early dawn. We had fought all night, not two hours.

Suddenly all was quiet. The fighting was over. The Chinese were withdrawing while they still had the cover of darkness.

I had made it through my first action. Alive. Unharmed

I said a silent prayer, thanking God for that. I felt no euphoria. No relief. A part of me was too numb to feel anything except a recognition that it was over. I had made it through my first real action, and I hadn't let anyone down. I had worried about that.

Gradually I became conscious of a dampness against my face and skin. I glanced down, thinking I must have done a lot of sweating during the night. Then I noticed some strange-looking stuff on the sleeves of my fatigues.

Staring at it, I said to Blackburn, "What the hell is this?" As I looked more closely at a larger piece, I didn't want to believe what I was seeing. It bristled with dark hair follicles.

"Oh, jeezus," Blackburn murmured. "That's a piece of skin with hair on it, Nick."

"Sweet Jesus, no." But I knew he was right. It was human. More than that, I knew it was from one of our guys. This was a fragment of somebody's skin.

I went crazy, frantically plucking off the bits of flesh. But they were everywhere — on my face, my clothes, my helmet, my hands, my flak jacket — everywhere. I was peppered with them. And the wetness, I knew it came from blood and body fluids.

"Jeezus, Nick, it's all over me, too," Blackburn whispered in horror.

My stomach rolled in revulsion, and I heaved my guts. When I finally stopped vomiting, I couldn't think about anything except getting this stuff off of me. But it wasn't on only me and Blackburn; it was all over the sandbags, the trench wall, everywhere.

More than anything, I wanted to rip off my clothes and throw them as far as I could, then stand under a hot shower and scrub away every trace of it. But that was impossible We were on the front line. I didn't have a spare uniform, an extra flak jacket or a helmet. With only five gallons of water issued per man, a shower was out of the question. I would have to live in these clothes and gear until we were rotated off the outpost.

I looked at Blackburn, "This is bad. This is real bad."

It was the understatement of all understatements.

Four

War is hell; I learned that last night. With the coming of full daylight, I found out that dealing with the mess afterwards is worse.

It turned out that the bits of flesh all over Blackburn and me had come from the two men scheduled to go stateside in a few days, — the ones who had hidden in the chink hole when the fighting started. An enemy artillery round had scored a direct hit on their hiding place, slamming inside of it and exploding, turning the chink hole into a firing chamber and blowing them all over the place.

Everybody said it was one of those freak accidents that sometimes happen during combat. It struck me that the word freak was an apt description, because I nearly freaked out when I realized what all those pieces were on me.

I couldn't help thinking about how close those two guys had been to getting out of Korea, away from this hell and back home.

They went home, all right. But there wasn't enough left of either man to put in a body bag.

That morning two guys went around the area with a poncho stretched between them. The rest of us picked up any body fragments we could find and put them in the poncho. It was a grim job that woke me up to the gruesome side of war.

Other than the loss of those two men, our casualties were minor, but the enemy dead littered the hillsides below Outpost Tom. Blackburn and I were assigned to one of the details that had the task of bringing the corpses up for the intelligence officers to search.

Fresh from collecting the remains of our own dead, I wasn't in any mood to feel much sympathy for theirs. The first two bodies we reached happened to be the Chinese soldiers that I had seen running

33

across the ditch. The whole post had opened fire on them. Their bodies were riddled with so many bullets that it was impossible to count how many times they had been shot thirty, forty times, maybe even more than that.

Last night, when they came up the hill, all hunched-over, these same Chinese soldiers had looked small and deadly. They still looked small, but a lot punier. Death had frozen the last expression on their faces, twisting their features into a mask of shock and pain.

But remembering those two men of ours, all I felt was anger. "You dirty sons-a-bitches, you had it coming."

And I kicked one of them in the back.

Even when I did it, I knew it wasn't right, but I couldn't help it.

When we picked up the first one, I noticed his arms were only half as big around as mine, but they were all wiry muscle. For as small as he was, he was a load to carry.

Blackburn noticed it, too. "This sonofabitch is heavy."

"I know." But I also thought I knew how the term dead weight had originated.

We hauled the body up to the trenches, went through his pockets, and found a photograph of his family and what appeared to be letters. These we turned over to the intelligence officer. He checked the body to make sure there wasn't any kind of booby trap on him. I thought it was a bit late to be doing that, considering we had just carried him up the hill. After the intelligence officer finished, the body was piled with the others that would eventually be taken to the rear and buried.

Before we headed back down the hill to bring up another one, I glanced at Blackburn. He looked pale and a little green.

"How're you doin'?" I asked.

"I think I'm going to be sick." He turned away and promptly threw up.

Personally I wondered how he had kept from doing it before now.

By that time, between the heat of the sun and the hot wind blowing on us, our clothes had dried. But there were stains all over them that resembled grease spots. Then it hit me that human flesh had fat in it, just like any animal. And our clothes, helmets and flak jackets were stained with it.

Once I noticed the darker greasy spots, I saw them every time I looked at Blackburn. It was odd the way I was quicker to see them on him than I was on myself. He told me it was the same with him.

It wasn't something we talked about much. We wanted to forget, but that was an impossibility. As long as we were on Outpost Tom, we had visible reminders of it in front of us all the time.

There wasn't much chance to rest that day. Even though I was dog-tired, I didn't really mind. In a way I dreaded the moment when I would have to shut my eyes for fear I would remember the sensation of those body parts on me. I wanted to forget that. And the only way I knew to do that was to get too tired to remember anything.

Late in the day, I heated up a can of C rations and walked over to squat beside Blackburn. I had my helmet on even though it felt like a steel weight on my head. I had made a point of wearing it all the time ever since an officer caught me without it in the latrine back on the MLR and royally chewed my ass out. I was slowly getting used to the heaviness of it.

After I had eaten a couple bites of food, Blackburn said, "I've been thinking, Nick."

"About what?"

"Us guys up here on the line — or any combat soldier in any war — do you realize that we are no different from a prisoner on death row. Those two guys up in that hole, it was their day to die. Tomorrow maybe it will be ours, or maybe we'll get a stay to fight another day." He poked at the food in his can. "People back home think we're just soldiers over here, but we're really on death row."

The more I thought about it, the more sense it made. "You're right, Blackburn. We are on death row."

I spent seven more days on Outpost Tom. Seven more days wearing those same stained clothes. On various nights during that time, we were put on one hundred per cent alert. The whole post opened fire, but we had no further contact with the enemy. Finally, on the ninth of May, we were relieved and sent back to the Wyoming Line.

Bob from Ohio was one of the first people I saw after I came off line. He walked up to me, wearing a big grin that showed those Army teeth of his. "Hello, Nick. Glad to see you back. How was it?"

"How was it? Look at these goddamned grease spots on my flak jacket."

"Where'd they come from?"

I told him.

He looked at me, this time without smiling. "That is bad shit Nick."

"Yeah. I'm having a problem with them. Me and Blackburn, both," I said. "Sometimes we look at each other and don't even talk about it."

Truth to tell, I didn't want to talk about it. The problem was — I couldn't forget it.

But I finally got a much-needed shower and a new set of fatigues as well as a hot meal, although just being away from Tom helped.

On our second night off of Tom, all of us on the machine gun crew headed out to see the movie being shown. Along the way, I spotted the location of the 'moonbeam', that old World War II searchlight.

It sat high atop a hill there on the Wyoming Line, silhouetted against the night sky, aimed at the slope on Outpost Tom, ready to illuminate it if necessary. It was an oddly comforting sight.

But comfort and ease were not the order of the night. About halfway through the movie, enemy artillery started firing from long range. I heard that now-distinctive whistle of an incoming round and ducked, but I never got off of my steel helmet. Blackburn, Pendleton, and the others did the same.

It exploded somewhere nearby, but not close enough to stop the movie. As long as the film continued to run, I intended to stay there and watch it. More rounds whistled in, but none of them landed anywhere near us.

Once the movie was over, we all headed back to our tent. As we got closer, I noticed a bunch of MPs standing around it.

"What the hell is going on? What are they doing here?" I wondered out loud.

"Good question," Corporal Pendleton was as puzzled as the rest of us.

It didn't take us long to find out. One of the artillery rounds had hit our tent and blown our cots, our duffel bags and everything else to smithereens. As I stared at the mess, I had a cold, eerie feeling in the pit of my stomach.

"Do you realize how lucky we are?" I said to Blackburn.

"Don't you know it. If we hadn't gone to that movie . . . " He let the rest trail off.

But he didn't have to say any more than that. We were all thinking the same thing. Right then, I said a silent prayer thanking God for sparing me. In Korea, I did a lot more praying than I had ever done before.

Even though we never thought we had anything to worry about on the Wyoming Line, sleep wasn't easy to come by that night. In the distance we could hear the thunder of continuing artillery bombardment.

The scuttlebutt had it that Outpost Harry was under attack. From the sounds of it, I knew they had to be catching hell. And I remembered that scared helpless feeling on Tom when the shells were exploding all around me. It was hard not to be glad someone else was on Harry and not me.

The next morning we woke up to bad news. During the night, the Red Chinese Army had launched a massive assault against Outpost Harry. There had been hand-to-hand fighting in the trenches before their attack was finally repulsed.

Evacuation of the dead and wounded was underway, and reinforcements were ordered to the outpost. My machine gun unit was among the replacements ordered in, abruptly cutting short our stay on the Wyoming Line.

We hastily assembled and piled into a deuce-and-a-half. Before long, we were headed north along a dirt road to the outpost.

Shortly after we left the Wyoming Line, the road snaked along a narrow gap between a series of tree-studded hills, following the path of a creek bed that wound through them. Nowhere was there any big open valley like I'd seen at Outpost Tom. The terrain here was hilly and rough, a portent of what I was to see on Harry.

Outpost Harry occupied a tall hill that was part of a larger hill mass held by the enemy, called Star Hill. Harry's superior elevation made it possible for the United Nations troops to have an early warning of any approach by the Chinese.

Our deuce-and-a-half took us to an area somewhere to the rear of Outpost Harry. We were told that enemy artillery made it impossible for them to transport us any closer. To reach the outpost, we would have to go the rest of the way on foot.

We climbed out of the deuce-and-a-half and moved into a timbered area away from the road. The plan was to use the trees as cover for our approach to Harry.

BOOM! BOOM! BOOM!

In rapid succession, artillery shells landed all along the road next to us, each explosion throwing up clouds of dust and smoke. Through the trees, I watched while enemy artillery shells walked that crooked road with an accuracy that was uncanny.

At that moment I realized just how damned good those Chinese manning the artillery were. And I was damned glad the deuce-and-a-half had let us off where it had, or we would be on that road.

Just about the time I started to thank God for that, the enemy artillery switched its target area and started dropping its rounds on the timbered area where we were. With the first blast, I dived for the nearest cover. My helmet went sailing. I scrambled to reach it, crammed it on my head and held it there while I hid behind a rock about six inches high.

That rock was about the only cover the area offered. And there were plenty of guys flattened beside rocks even smaller.

Round after round pierced the canopy of tree branches, raining down a shower of shredded leaves and wood splinters. Still more shells crashed into the timber, landing so close that the ground shook, so violently that I was lifted off it. The explosions came almost on top of each other until I was practically bouncing from the impact of them.

"Our Father, which art in heaven, hallowed be thy name." I never prayed so fast and so earnestly in my life, rushing to get out all the words to the Lord's Prayer, then never stopping, just repeating it over and over again like a mantra.

Somewhere close by, a guy yelled, "I'm hit! I'm hit!"

I stole a peek from under my helmet just as he scrambled to his feet and took off. There he went, hopping as fast as a guy could on one leg back towards the MLR. All the while shells exploded on either side of him. If I hadn't been so scared myself, I probably would have laughed at the sight.

The shelling lasted for what seemed like an eternity. When it finally lifted, the silence was almost eerie. A little dazed and shaken I got slowly to my feet and looked around to make sure Blackburn, Pendleton, and the others were all right, too. Smoke and dust hung in those woods like a fog, and the air reeked of gunpowder.

Once I saw that my buddies were okay, I made a better check of myself. That's when I noticed that I had big, purple-red splotches of blood all over my hands and arms. They had a bruise-like swelling, a little like a blood blister. The other guys had them, too. The medic told us that they were caused by the concussions from the exploding the shells. It was the first time I had ever heard of such a thing.

With the enemy barrage over, we reassembled and once again started for the outpost. Late that afternoon, we reached a supply point near the foot of Harry. There we were to wait for the cover of darkness to make our way up the communication trench to the outpost itself.

The waiting was hard on the nerves. I didn't want to think about what the night might bring. At the same time, I couldn't help remembering that the previous night the Chinese had reached the trenches on Harry. Nothing like that had happened while I was on Outpost Tom.

I kept wondering if the Chinese would attack again, or if their failure to take the hill last night had convinced them not to try again.

The possibility that I might see some hand-to-hand fighting made me wonder just how much protection our flak jackets offered. I decided to find out.

When I took off my flak jacket, Blackburn looked at me and frowned. "What are you doing?"

"I'm going to find out if this thing can really stop a bullet?"

I walked over to a half-rotted log well clear of the others, draped my flak jacket over it, stepped back a few paces and fired. When I checked the jacket, I saw that the bullet hadn't pierced it.

You don't know how happy that made me. I put that flak jacket back on. Just wearing it gave me a feeling of safety that I can't describe.

When the light faded, we moved out, single file, heading up the trench. As an ammo bearer, I had the ammunition belts for our machine gun slung over my shoulders John Wayne-style, leaving my hands free to carry my carbine.

The previous night's mortar and artillery bombardment by the Chinese had reduced the depth of the trenches to a mere four feet, even less than that in some places. There hadn't been time to remove all the enemy dead, and their bodies were stacked along the trench like piles of sandbags.

The ground was slick underfoot, and that odd, tinny smell of blood and rotting flesh hung in the air. I could hear the buzzing of flies that swarmed over the corpses. Rats were everywhere, scurrying and squeaking, watching with beady eyes as we passed, with the idle interest of someone looking at a future meal. I kicked at any of them that came within range of my boot.

Suddenly one of my ammo belts snagged on something. When I glanced back to see what it was caught on, a flare shot up, lighting the trenches. I found myself staring at a Chinese corpse sitting in the trench, one arm upraised in death.

My ammo belt was hooked around his hand. The top half of his head, from his eyebrows up, had been sheared off. I was looking at his brains.

The sight freaked me out. I thought — You want this fucking ammo you take it. I shed that belt so fast it probably set a record. I didn't care. I just wanted away from him.

We finally reached the main trench on Harry and took up our assigned position. This time we didn't have the shelter of a bunker. It had gotten blown to hell the night before.

We didn't waste time setting up our water-cooled machine gun on the bank of the trench. Pendleton manned the gun while Blackburn and I took up defensive positions on either side of it

The hill sloped steeply away from us, dipped into a fold in the hill mass, then rose again on the other side — the enemy side. It was all woods over there, and thickly shadowed.

I already had my bayonet locked on my carbine. We had no way of knowing whether we would see a repeat of last night's hand-to-hand fighting, but we were prepared just in case.

I settled into my position and lit a cigarette to kill time, careful to keep my hand cupped around it. As I took a second puff, I heard music. Big band music. It seemed to be coming from the hillside fronting us. The music was all scratchy, like an old record, but the words were sung in Chinese. The tune was familiar, though. It took me a minute to recognize the song "I Ain't Got No Yo-Yo."

"Where's that music coming from, Corp?" I asked Pendleton.

"The Chinese have loud speakers mounted in those trees across the way," Pendletonn told me. "Pretty soon, they'll start talking to us."

He was right. After a couple songs, a voice came over the speakers, broadcasting in perfect English, telling us how much fun they had had last night. The guy rattled off a dozen or so American names, telling us that they hoped they would have as much fun with us, laughing and saying that maybe they'll capture us, too. More big band music was played, sung in Chinese the same as before. Afterwards the guy talked about more of our men who had been on Harry the night before.

It was an eerie mind game, the kind that messed with your head. It got on my nerves until I wanted to scream for them to shut up! At the same time I didn't want to give the Chinese the satisfaction of knowing that they were getting to me. So I gritted my teeth and listened.

After what seemed like an eternity, the music and talking finally stopped. But oddly the silence seemed worse.

It was close to midnight and everything was black as hell. I was hunkered against the wall of the trench, waiting like everyone else, but not sure what was coming. Something told me if there was ever a hell on earth, it was right there on Outpost Harry.

Sitting there in that inky blackness, seeing the sheen of the bayonet I'd fixed to my rifle, waiting and wondering if there would be a repeat of the Chinese assault, I was about as scared a twenty-year old can be.

Nobody was doing much talking. And my nerves were stretched tighter than a tenor string.

Suddenly the silence was shattered by the eerie blare of a bugle coming from the darkness beyond the trench. At almost the same instant, a green flare arced across the night sky, and the air screamed with the distinctive whine of incoming artillery rounds.

Before the ground shook with the first explosion, I had a glimpse of hunched-over figures, bathed in the weird green glow of the dying flare, as they flooded out of the trees on the opposite slope in a human wave. It was a sight straight out of a nightmare, except it was real.

Those bastards were attacking!

For a split second, I wondered what the hell I was doing there? How in the world had I gotten myself into this situation? But there wasn't much time for thinking.

Just about then Pendleton opened up with a machine gun burst. I stole a peek over the top as one of our single-engine spotter planes shot off a flare that illuminated the hillside. Hundreds of Chinese were rushing toward our position like so-many ants, using the artillery barrage to cover their advance.

Just about then, a shell exploded close by. I ducked, but shrapnel from it struck the jacket to our water-cooled machine gun, splintering it.

I yelled to Pendleton, "Was the machine gun hit, Corp?"

"I can't tell."

But he was already stripping the ammunition belt from it and grabbing a carbine. I knew he figured the barrel was damaged and didn't want to risk firing it to find out. I didn't blame him.

With the machine gun inoperative and artillery shells still whistling in, Pendleton and his assistant gunner spread out along the trench. Another shell landed near us, exploding in a geyser of soil and rock. I ducked under the shower of pelting dirt clods and rock, holding my helmet. I figured that as long as I heard the whistle of an incoming shell, I was okay. It was the one I didn't hear that would get me.

The relentless barrage made it nearly impossible to do more than snap off a shot or two at the bent-over targets coming up the slope. And with the image of that dead Chinese's brains still fresh in my mind, I wasn't eager to poke my head over the trench to look, not with those rounds falling so fast and furious. The entire hill was cloaked in a haze of smoke and dust, all of it eerily illuminated by the flares from the spotter planes.

Another shell slammed into the hill above me, unleashing a deluge of dirt into the trench. Ducking again, I hugged the side of the embankment until the rain of debris eased off, then lifted myself up.

There, in front of me, just coming over the sandbagged lip of the trench was a Red Chinese soldier, dressed in a quilted jacket and armed with a burp gun.

I shouted a warning, "Blackburn!"

"Get him now, Nick!"

Yelling, I plunged my bayonet into him, jamming it all the way to the hilt. Worried that he would fall on me, I gave a sideways jerk, then pulled the trigger, blowing him off the blade without ever trying to pull it out.

He tumbled to the bottom of the trench, falling in a sprawl. I kicked him to make sure he was dead, then kicked him again for no reason other than he was dead and I wasn't.

I noticed the blade of my bayonet was all red, and shiny with his blood. I wiped it off on his quilted jacket, figuring why the hell not, it was his fucking blood.

The Bible says, "Thou shall not kill." But this was war. If I hadn't killed him, he would have killed me — or Blackburn, Pendleton or one of the others.

Somehow I knew that there wasn't room in combat for a conscience.

The enemy was dead. I had killed him. At that moment, I didn't feel the slightest bit of remorse. My instructor during basic training had been right; if there were to be any recriminations, they would come at a later date. But his death made me realize one thing — I was mortal. At that moment, I think I grew up. I wasn't a twenty-year old punk kid anymore; I was a man.

Blackburn bent over the body, then turned to me. "Jeeze, Nick. Look."

I finally took my first good look at the face of the dead Chinese soldier. He was young, just a kid, maybe in his teens. And I was suddenly an older and wiser twenty.

"Oh, shit, here's another one, Nick."

I swung my weapon around to fire, but Blackburn had already turned to meet him, squeezing off a round before stabbing the guy with a bayonet.

Now we had two bodies at our feet. Working together, Blackburn and I heaved them over the trench bank and out of our way.

If two of the enemy had made it up the hill, common sense told me more were on the way. But the ground sloped away so steeply below our position that there was no way to see how close the enemy might be without exposing myself. But I knew I had to do something, give some kind of supporting fire.

Scared and pumped with adrenaline all at the same time, I decided to risk getting my hand shot up rather than my head. I poked my carbine over the top of the trench and fired off a short burst.

Wham, wham, wham, wham.

Bullets came zinging back, striking the wall of the trench behind me. I fired again. Instantly bullets whipped over my head.

'Jeezus, they zeroed in on me awfully quick,' I thought, and peeked over the trench to see how close they were.

That's when I noticed the concertina post directly below my position. I realized, then, that my own bullets had been ricocheting off the post and flying back at me.

I decided that firing blind was not a smart move. I could have been my own casualty!

I leaned against the side of the trench, trying to come up with another plan. Suddenly I felt something hot land on my leg. I looked, and there was a long and jagged artillery round lying against it.

The shell must have finned out above me and fallen harmlessly. I stared at it, realizing that it could have very easily blown up and taken off my whole leg. It was a miracle that it hadn't. At that moment, I knew I had a guardian angel watching over me. And I was quick to thank God for sending him because that thing scared the shit out of me — literally.

But I was still faced with the same dilemma — how to fight back? The answer came to me.

I yelled to Blackburn, shouting to make myself heard over the steady racket of explosions and gunfire, "I'm going for grenades."

I worked my way along the trench to the ammunition bunker, grabbed a case of grenades and carried them back to our position. When I opened up the case, it was full of smooth-shelled grenades, not the usual, dimple-sided pineapple grenades.

I didn't know if they were phosphorous or smoke grenades, but I thought what the hell, they were better than nothing and might cause some confusion.

I pulled the pin on the first one and lobbed it over the trench. It exploded with a very satisfying and resounding BOOM!

I picked up another one, and Blackburn joined me. We tossed grenade after grenade, dropping some over the side to roll down the hill and hurling the rest. It didn't seem to matter how many Chinese were killed, there were still more coming at us. As soon as that case was emptied, I went for another.

The grenades in that case were almost gone when somebody yelled, "The hill's been taken by the Chinese! We have to get outta here!"

Swinging around in panic, I looked up the trench, half expecting to see a horde of Chinese swarming toward me. But I only saw our own guys. I wasn't sure whether we should pull out or what.

Suddenly the air started screaming with in-coming rounds, and I hit the deck. The ground quaked with the aftershock of each explosion. It didn't take long to figure out that we were being bombarded by our own artillery. And with vicious accuracy.

Logic told me that if we were getting shelled by our own artillery, the Chinese must have overrun the rest of the outpost.

A major crawled into our trench area and shouted, "The fucking Chinese haven't taken this hill. We're still here, aren't we? Just stay in your position, and I'll see about getting this damned artillery off of us."

Minutes after the barrage of friendly artillery lifted, word filtered down the trench that the Chinese had taken one of our bunkers and barricaded themselves in it. Holes were being punched in a fifty-five gallon drum of gasoline. The plan was to let the gasoline run into the bunker, then set fire to it.

Off to my right, orange-red flames shot into the sky with a sudden roar. Seconds later, the wind swept the stench of burnt flesh, mixed with gasoline fumes, to our section.

Beside me, Blackburn murmured, "They were burned alive. That's gotta be a helluva way to die."

"A helluva way," I agreed. At the same time, it reminded me of the comment Blackburn had made a couple days before — that we were all on death row, never knowing if this was the day we lived or died.

"Look. It's morning already." Blackburn nodded toward the east where first blush of dawn streaked the sky.

Just like on Outpost Tom, the night of fighting has passed with an odd swiftness. Already the Chinese had begun their withdrawal, leaving their dead behind.

Five

Later that morning our platoon sergeant came to our section of the trench. "Load up," he said. "Our replacements have arrived. Let's get the hell off this hill."

Without a doubt that was the most beautiful order I had ever heard.

The floor of the trench was slick with bloody mud and alive with rats. The entire place reeked with the smell of dead bodies that had been dumped on the other side of the sandbags, including the one I had killed.

None of us wasted much time gathering up our weapons. During the night's fighting, we had managed to scavenge quite an assortment in addition to the carbines and .45s we'd been issued. The sergeant picked up the damaged water-cooled machine gun that the shrapnel had put out of commission.

"Why are you bothering to haul that down, Sarge?" someone asked. "It doesn't work. The water jacket's been blown."

"Even if it's inoperable, it has to be removed. That's the orders," the sergeant reminded him. "We don't leave anything behind that the enemy might be able to salvage if they ever got their hands on it."

It was standard Army procedure. I saw the sense in it, but that machine gun was still a piece of junk as far as I was concerned.

Loaded down with our weapons, we made our way along the trenches to the holding area at the base. We were a dirty, scruffy-looking group, coming off the adrenaline-high of combat. A mind-numbing weariness had set in. We were covered with the blood and grime of battle, and we smelled like it, too, but nobody seemed to notice. I guess we were all too tired to care, and the odor was too common.

By this time, nearly all the wounded had been taken off Outpost Harry. The more critically injured had been evacuated to the rear and coptered to the closest M.A.S.H. unit.

But details were still bringing out some of our dead. I saw some bodies lying on the ground, prior to being taken to the rear. I couldn't help looking at them, conscious that it could just as easily have been me lying there with my dog tag between my teeth.

Two guys arrived, toting another body. One glance at that skinny, lifeless figure, all white and little and I knew it was Bob from Ohio. He was dead, killed on Harry.

My throat knotted up, choking back feelings that I couldn't put a name to. Memories flashed through my mind of our time together on the ship, the way we'd both felt like John Wayne on that landing barge coming into Inch'on Harbor, and those Army teeth he'd been so proud of. I just hoped to God those teeth were sturdy enough to keep a grip on his dog tag.

Orders came for our platoon to assemble, prior to heading to the rear. Wearily, we fell in, lining up in formation, shoulder to shoulder, our weapons in hand.

Suddenly, there was the loud report of a gunshot, and we all dropped to the dirt, certain there was an enemy sniper about. Everywhere people scurried for cover.

But no more shots came.

As I got to my feet, someone said, "Jeeze, it's the Sarge. He's been hit."

Our company medic raced over, but there was nothing Doc could do. The sergeant was dead. There had been a live round in the firing chamber of that worthless, damned machine gun he had carried off Outpost Harry.

A machine gun has no trigger guard. When the sergeant set the butt of the gun on the ground, the trigger obviously hit something, firing the round in the chamber. The bullet had traveled up through his armpit, into his chin and out his brains.

That useless piece of junk had killed him. He had died for horrible nothing. We had just come through a night of hell, and he had gotten killed by a scrapped weapon! It wasn't right.

The injustice of it made me furious. I wanted to strike out at somebody, hit something, but I knew it was futile. As futile as his death.

We slipped his dog tag into his mouth, made sure his teeth came together on the groove along the top of it, then carried him over to lay with the rest of the dead from Harry.

But his death had been such an utter waste. The anger over it stayed with me. Most of the time I kept it bottled up, only with Blackburn did I let some of it out.

Leaving our sergeant to be hauled away with the rest of the dead, we were moved to a blocking position a short distance to the rear of the MLR.

Blackburn nudged my arm. "They've got hot coffee and donuts over there. You want some, Nick?"

"Sure. Why not?"

Coffee sounded better to me than donuts until I bit into one. I chewed on it and tried not to think about Bob or the sergeant. But the thought of them stayed in the back of my mind. It was the first time I had known the soldiers who had been killed. The others had always been strangers to me. But I couldn't say that about Bob or the Sarge.

I washed down the last of the donut with some coffee, refilled my cup and drifted away from the table to have a cigarette. I noticed our company medic standing off by himself, scarfing down a donut. Doc, we called him, except during a firefight. Then, if we needed him, we hollered "Shotgun!" so the enemy wouldn't know we were calling for a medic and zero in on him when he came to help.

From the looks of him, he'd had a helluva night, too. It was odd, but I couldn't remember anyone yelling for him. Yet he was covered with blood, even the hand holding the donut was smeared with it. Like the rest of us, he didn't give a tinker's damn about how dirty he was. There was hot coffee and donuts and he was going to have some.

Every night for the next six days, we were on one hundred per cent alert, awake and ready in the event we were called in for support.

On the night of June 17th, after eight days of fighting, the Chinese made their last assault on Harry. Just like every other time, they were thrown back. Finally, late on the 18th of June, we were relieved by the 65th Infantry and sent back to the Wyoming Line.

During one of our first days on the Wyoming Line, we attended a class to instruct us in the use of a new hand grenade, soon to be introduced to replace the old pineapple one.

48

I took one look at the smooth-skinned grenade the officer was holding and said, "This is dumb."

He stiffened a little. "What do you mean?"

"We had grenades just like that one on Outpost Harry. Blackburn and I must have gone through two cases of them."

"This is your new grenade." He went on to explain about the steel spring down the center of it and the mooning effect that would be created. He claimed that the new grenade would explode into smaller pieces that would penetrate deeper than the old pineapple grenade.

But it boiled down to the same thing — you pulled the pin, gave it a throw, and it went BOOM!

But the Army wasn't about to neglect our education. They schooled us in such things as the recoilless rifle and the use of C-3 explosives.

With the explosives, we were taught how to dig the hole, determine the angle of the blow, and how to put in the charge. When they were ready to set the charge off, they would yell, "Everybody get back! Fire in the hole! Fire in the hole!"

To which someone would always respond, hollering, "Well, piss on it."

Nighttime, it was different. At night, we drank beer, played cards, shot craps, caught a USO show if one came in, or went to a movie in camp. Audie Murphy starred in a lot of the films they showed, which was logical considering the Fifteenth was his old regiment.

But my favorite movie star was Debbie Reynolds. I was in love with that girl, and I wasn't shy about saying so. To me, she was the most gorgeous woman there was.

One night while we were sitting around drinking beer, I got to talking about her. Before I knew it, somebody came up with the bright idea that we should write and ask Debbie for an autographed picture.

Somebody grabbed some paper. Someone else scrounged up a pen. Then we all gathered together, Blackburn, myself, Pendleton, and one or two other guys, and composed a letter to her.

'Dear Debbie,' we wrote.

'We are with the Fifteenth Regiment, Audie Murphy's old outfit, stationed in Korea. We are sitting here on a machine gun a thousand miles from home. We have seen every one of your movies.' And we wrote down every one we could remember. 'All of us agree that you are a very beautiful woman. Would you take pity on a bunch of lonely machine gunners and send us a pin-up photo of you? That would make us happier than you could possibly know.'

Then we closed it off and signed our names to it. We had no idea what her address was, so we just wrote on the envelope: Debbie Reynolds, Hollywood, California.

We all laughed about that. It wasn't much of an address. But, for the hell of it, we mailed it anyhow. There was always the chance someone in the postal department would forward our letter to the correct address. It might take several months or more, but she could still get it.

The next day someone brought a copy of "The Stars and Stripes" back to our tent. It contained an article about the second night of fighting on Outpost Harry, the night I was there.

According to "The Stars and Stripes", the outpost had been assaulted by a force of approximately 1,500 Chinese troops, making it roughly regimental strength. (That number was eventually adjusted to 2,850, which meant that there were fifteen Chinese to every one of us that night. In all, after eight days of fighting on Harry, the Chinese suffered an estimated 1,670 dead and 3,800 wounded, while our casualties were 102 dead, 533 wounded and 44 missing in action for the same period.) The article went on to say that, for a brief period, the Chinese had succeeded in cutting off the outpost before they were forced to retreat.

I guess I had always known the fighting on Harry had been savage and desperate. But during the battle, I had only known about the fighting along my section of the trenches. There hadn't been any way for me to know the whole picture. It was probably just as well that I hadn't known. But reading that article made me realize just how damned lucky I had been. I thanked God for that and for seeing me safely through it.

Then I spotted the paragraph near the bottom of the article, one that quoted the Eighth Army as saying some 94,000 rounds enemy artillery and mortar were fired along the frontline positions during the previous twenty-four hour period.

"Did you see this, Blackburn?" I pointed to the paragraph. "How in hell does the Army know how many rounds were fired? Did you see anybody up there on Harry counting them as they were coming in, because I sure as hell didn't?"

"That would have been a sight, wouldn't it?" He grinned, then looked in the air and pantomimed "There's one. There's two. Is that an artillery round or a mortar, Nick? It came down a little too quick for me to tell."

"It was a mortar. Take my word for it."

We must have joked about that for a week. Then I found out that Army regulations require the filing of a report after every shelling, detailing the number and caliber of all in-coming shells and an inspection of their craters. It was a job that some junior officer usually got stuck doing. The damned Army actually did try to count them.

One night while we were still on the Wyoming line, I woke up in a cold sweat. I was back on Outpost Tom with those bits of human flesh all over me. I could feel them, the warmth of them, and the wetness. The horror and revulsion I felt was just as strong as the night it happened.

In desperation, I shook Blackburn awake. "My skin's crawling," I whispered.

I didn't have to say more than that. He rolled out of his cot.

"I know what you're feeling, Nick," he said. "It happened to me the other night."

I rubbed at my arms, trying to get rid of the sensation. "I still can't get those pieces of skin out of my system."

Blackburn nodded in understanding. "When I got up the other night, I ended up going to the latrine and throwing up."

"Well, I can control my stomach, but my skin — it's just crawling. I don't want anyone else to know how I feel because . . . "

Blackburn finished the sentence that I couldn't. "Yeah, the other guys will probably think we're a couple of chicken shits if they found out."

"I wanted to tell you, though."

"The other night I wanted to tell you, too, Nick. But I wasn't sure whether you'd make fun of me."

"You don't have to worry about that. Something like this isn't funny."

"I know."

Just knowing I could talk to him made it easier somehow. I felt close to Blackburn. Not like he was my brother or anything like that. It was something different. Korea had united us in a way that I knew I could never describe. It freed me to say things I probably would never have said to another living soul.

"You know those grease spots — we washed them out of our flak jackets, but . . . I can still feel the wetness on my face."

"Yeah." Blackburn nodded. "I thought we could get rid of it once we got out of those clothes. But we can't."

"I guess not."

"Want to play some cards?" Blackburn knew there wasn't any way I could go back to sleep. Not yet. Not for awhile.

We played a lot of cards late at night. There was an unspoken pact in our group that, if any of us started feeling low or a little homesick, you woke one of the others up to keep you company. I ended up playing a lot of cards and shooting a lot of craps in Korea. I also drank a lot of beer and smoked a lot of cigarettes, too.

And what a small world Korea turned out to be while I was there. One day a guy came up to me and introduced himself.

"My name's Bruce Farris. I understand you're from Council Bluffs, Iowa. I used to live there. You wouldn't happen to know Dale Hambo would you?"

"I know Dale."

By the time we finished trading names, it turned out that we both knew some of the same people.

Farris was in communications, which meant he ran the communication wire strung between the concertina posts. It sounded like an easy job until he pointed out that he had to re-string any lines that were blown out by shellfire — sometimes while the shells were still coming out of the sky.

Like me, Farris wasn't averse to a little gambling. Come payday, the two of us pooled our resources and set up a blackjack game, no limits. Farris handled the banking side, and I did the dealing.

When we finally called it quits for the night, we ended up with nearly eight hundred dollars to split between us. It was a very profitable evening for a couple of soldiers.

We hung around the Wyoming line, waiting for whatever came next, confident of one thing — the Army would keep us busy.

Armed with C-3 explosives, we were sent out along the Wyoming line to do a bunch of dog work. We spent the entire day digging in and blowing out, — and broiling in the hot sun with Korea's incessant, hot wind hurling dust in our faces.

By the time we returned to camp that day, I was beat. I always thought that Iowa had the corner on hot summers, but it was nothing compared to the dust and heat of Korea with its blazing sun and the putrid stench from its rice paddies. There never seemed to be any relief from either one.

As I headed for our tent, my feet dragging, some guy yelled at me, "Hey, Nick, your brother's down at the command post."

Stopping, I frowned. "I don't have a brother over here." Then it hit me that this was some kind of practical joke. But I was too hot, too tired, and too sweaty to see the humor of it. "Quit trying to pull my leg."

The guy shrugged. "I'm not. A guy claiming to be your brother is up at CP."

"For your information, I don't have any brother who is qualified to be over here." I was tired enough to be just a bit testy.

"If you say so. Just the same, there's a guy at CP who's telling a different story."

He walked off. I stood there a minute, then decided I might as well find out what the hell was going on. So, I headed up to the command post.

When I got there, there stood my sister's brother-in-law, Kinnaman. My mouth dropped open about a mile.

"What the hell are you doing here?" I grabbed his hand and slapped his shoulder.

Maybe he was shoestring family, but he was still family.

"When I came in, they asked me where I wanted to be and where I was from. When I told them I was from Iowa, they said they had a guy from Iowa here. I said his name wouldn't happen to be Nick Dick, would it? When they told me it was, I said that wherever he was, that's where I want to be. And here I am."

I took him back to our company area, still amazed that he had ended up here. It was such a wild coincidence that he had first shown up at the same basic training camp, then been assigned to my outfit I here in Korea.

After Kinnaman had caught me up on all the news from home, he asked how things had been going over here. I told him a little about the action I'd seen on Outpost Tom, and the trench fighting on Harry. But I could tell he was too combat-green to appreciate how truly hellacious it had been, so I changed the subject.

"How are you fixed for cash?" I asked instead. "If you've got any to spare for gambling, we're having a game tonight."

I was running low myself. Somehow, my winnings from the blackjack game with Farris had managed to vanish into thin air.

"I've got a couple bucks."

Two dollars wasn't much for what I had in mind. "You gamble with it."

"I don't think so."

"How about giving it to me and I'll put it with what I have? Maybe we can win enough to buy us some saki beer and do some celebrating."

Lady Luck smiled on us. We walked away from the game with enough money to buy two cases of the Korean beer.

We hauled the beer to a mountain stream that wandered through the camp. There was a place where it widened out into a good-sized pool. Like most of the water in Korea, it was brownish in color and carried a faint odor of raw sewage. But it was also cold. Cold enough to chill our beer.

Kinnaman and I started drinking. It didn't take long for word to spread that we were having a party. Soon we had a crowd at stream-side. One guy showed up with a bottle of Russian vodka.

"Here." He offered it to me. "Have a drink, Nick."

This was free liquor. I wasn't about to turn it down. I took the bottle from him, tipped it up and took a long swig, then washed it down with some more beer.

When I woke up the next morning, I was on my cot, drenched to the skin. I piled out of my sleeping bag, convinced I'd been too drunk to get up and go to the latrine.

"Oh shit," I muttered. "I must have pissed all over myself."

Blackburn grinned. "Hell no, you didn't. You jumped in the pond and started opening up beer cans and passing them out to everyone who came by."

"I did?"

"Yup."

"All I remember is downing a big swallow of vodka."

"I'm not surprised. That stuff was one hundred proof."

While I dug out some dry clothes and changed into them, Blackburn filled me in on the rest of the night's happenings. When he finished, I told him about Kinnaman being a shirttail relation of mine, and about the way he had followed me first to basic training, then here to Korea.

"I tried to tell him about Outposts Tom and Harry, but — Do you know what he said? 'What the hell. I came over here to fight.' He had such a cocky attitude, like none of that wasn't any big deal. I don't know why, but it just hit me wrong.

"I know what you mean." Blackburn said. "A lot of the new guys have that attitude. Maybe all of us did to some extent when we first got here. But you can bet, they'll change their tune in a hurry when they get their first taste of combat."

"That's for damned sure."

* * *

In the early part of July, word came down that our outfit was moving off line to a reserve area a few miles to the rear. We were ordered to present all our weapons.

During our stint on Outpost Harry, we had collected quite an assortment. We had four rocket launchers, a Thompson machine gun, a half dozen other machine guns including a .35 caliber one we called a grease gun, and a Browning Automatic Rifle. This was all in addition to the carbines, .45 pistols, a water-cooled and an air-cooled machine gun , plus the M-1s that we were supposed to have.

The officer took one look at our cache of weapons and said, "Jesus Christ! What are you guys going to do when we take all of these away from you?"

"You aren't really going to take them from us, are you?" somebody protested.

"We sure as hell are. You won't need this much fire power where you're going, just the equipment you were originally issued."

They took away our four rocket launchers, the extra machine guns, the Thompson and the Browning Automatic, then stripped the ammo bearers of their .45 pistols. Somehow I managed to hang on to my pistol even though I wasn't officially a machine gunner at that point. Then we were ordered to turn in our flak jackets as well.

No flak jackets meant no combat for us. And that was one beautiful thought.

After our duffel bags were loaded, we climbed into the waiting Jeeps. I happened to have some saki beer stashed in the tent. Determined not to leave it behind, I managed to stuff all the cans in the water tank, mounted in back of the Jeep.

Before we pulled out, an officer came by, checking to verify that all our canteens were full as well as the tank. When he reached our Jeep, he lifted the lid on the tank and said, "Oh, shit."

That's all he said, just "oh, shit", closed the lid and moved on to the next Jeep. I knew that if we had been heading in any direction except to the rear, my beer would have been long gone.

Not long after we arrived at the reserve area, a rumor started circulating that we would be going to Koje Island to guard prisoners. It sounded like a sweet assignment. According to the scuttlebutt, orders to that effect were supposed to arrive any day.

Only one order came through. Blackburn had been chosen to attend officer's training school. I knew it was a great opportunity for Blackburn, but I also knew I was going to miss that skinny guy with glasses.

Klang was his replacement. From Washington state, Klang was under six foot tall and a little on the stocky side, like me. He was a likeable guy. But the strong bond that comes from shared experiences in combat wasn't there — yet.

Six

On the night of July 13, 1953, all hell broke loose along the front line.

I didn't know it at the time, but Singhman Rhee, the Korean president, had outraged the Chinese by, among other things, arbitrarily releasing thousands of prisoners of war. By doing so, Rhee had totally ignored the agreed procedure that had been hammered out between the Communists and the United Nations representatives at the peace table in Panmunjom

In retaliation for Rhee's actions, the Chinese launched a massive attack, throwing an estimated seven divisions of Chinese Communist Forces against a single division of the ROK Army. (ROK is an acronym for the Republic of Korea; they were on our side.)

Seven divisions against one. I guess I don't have to say any more than that.

By the morning of the July 14th, the ROKs were awash in a sea of Red Chinese. The Fifteenth — the Can Do — Regiment was among the units ordered forward to halt the flood.

Only the top brass knew what we would be up against that rainy morning when a convoy of empty deuce-and-a-halfs roared into camp. Orders flew.

"Grab you weapons and ammunition! There's a hole in our line. Everybody in the trucks."

When they said 'everybody, there were no exceptions. Cooks, dishwashers, — the Army didn't care what your job normally was. If you had on an Army uniform, they shoved a gun in your hands and pushed you into a truck.

We piled into those deuce-and-a-halfs while Dickerson, our new platoon sergeant from Georgia, raced to the motor pool. It was his job to get our Jeep, hook up the trailer and head to the ammunition dump to get our machine guns and ammunition.

As soon as our truck was loaded, the driver pulled out, gears grinding and the wheels slipping in the mud. Once we were on our way, the things we'd been told began to sink in — the Chinese had broken through our line. I remembered the hell of Outpost Harry with the Chinese
swarming up the hill and into the trenches. And here we were with no flak jackets.

Tension crept in, the kind of tension that comes from experience and the uncertainty of the hell that might be waiting. Something told me that if I ever needed God with me, I needed Him now.

Without even thinking, I started singing the first song that came to mind — "Onward Christian Soldiers". I wasn't singing for anybody else but myself. And I didn't give a damn if any of the others thought it was weird or silly.

Before I knew it, everybody in the truck joined in and sang with me. The guys in the troop carriers ahead and behind us heard the singing. Soon they were singing, too. There we were, crammed in the back of deuce-and-a-halfs plowing through a driving rain to who knows what, singing "Onward Christian Soldiers".

Maybe the song choice is a strange one. But we were soldiers heading into battle, just like the ones in the song. And this was one time none of us were ashamed to admit we believed in God, not the combat veterans or the green recruits. And we wanted Him with us.

The singing helped. I know it helped me, and I think it helped the others, too. In the silence that followed, there was only the steady rumble of the engine, the pelting downpour and the splash of tires to break it.

I remembered the tiny Bible my folks had given me before I left for Korea. I always carried it in my pocket, mostly out of respect for them. I took it out and leafed through the pages until I found the Twenty-third Psalm. I started reading it.

Somebody said, "Read it aloud, Nick."

So I did, sometimes losing my place as we bounced along the rutty road. But it didn't matter. I knew the psalm by heart.

"'The Lord is my shepherd; I shall not want.

'He maketh me to lie down in green pastures; he leadeth me beside the still waters.

'He restoreth my soul; He leadeth me in the paths of righteousness for His name's sake.

'Yea, though I walk through the valley of the shadow of death, I will fear no evil; for Thou art with me; Thy rod and Thy staff they comfort me.

'Thou preparest a table before me in the presence of mine enemies; Thou anointest my head with oil; my cup runneth over.

'Surely goodness and mercy shall follow me all the days of my life; and I will dwell in the house of the Lord for ever.'

"Amen."

After I finished, someone else began reciting the Lord's Prayer. Just about everybody joined in, some with and heads bowed and eyes closed, some just stared at the floorboards or outside at the falling rain, their voices low and subdued. And those who didn't lend their voice to the prayer listened quietly.

After that nobody did much talking.

Us guys singing and praying probably sounds schmaltzy, like some corny scene you'd see in a Hollywood B movie about war. But this wasn't make-believe; this was the way it really happened.

Anyway, we arrived at the rendezvous point and joined the teeming mass of activity as truck after truck disgorged their load of soldiers into the churned-up mud. This was the end of the line for the deuce-and-a-halfs. From here, the infantry would advance on foot.

Corporal Pendleton took off to locate our Jeep. In short order, he returned with it and the trailer loaded with our machine guns and ammo a canvas tarp stretched across it to protect it from the rain.

By the time I slogged through the mud to our waiting Jeep, I was damned glad that I was in Dog Company and not a foot soldier. Even with a poncho, I was soaked to the skin and the rain was still falling in buckets.

"Come on, Nick. Let's go," Pendleton shouted. "We're ready to pull out."

I climbed into the front of the Jeep while Klang crawled in the back. We took off, heading up a muddy road that led into the mountains in the Kumson sector.

"What's going on, Corp? Do you know?" I asked Pendleton.

"Scuttlebutt has it that the Chinese broke through the ROK lines and over-ran our Double Nickel artillery. Our guys are either dead or captured."

"Oh, shit," I said, but I wasn't sure if I was thinking of them or what it meant that we would be facing.

"I think you just described the situation, Nick," he replied.

I saw the grimness in his expression. I knew that, deep down, he was just as scared as I was, but I'd been in combat with him before. In a crisis, Pendleton was steady as a rock, mentally organized and in control. Klang was an unknown factor in our group since he'd never been in combat, but I knew how the corporal would react.

Turning, I glanced over my shoulder at the gear in the back of the Jeep. "Where's our flak jackets? Did you pick them up?"

"No," Pendleton replied.

"What do you mean — no? We're going to need them."

"I know we are," Pendleton said, as calm as you please. "But there weren't any jackets to get."

I was worried before, but I was really sweating it now. Here we were going into combat without flak jackets. I knew God had His work cut out for Him if He was going to get me through this one.

Then, for some reason, I noticed that there wasn't any sign of our duffel bags stowed in back.

"I turned to Pendleton. "Didn't you get our duffel bags?"

"Nope. They weren't there either."

"Shit. That means we don't have our fart sacks. And what the hell am I gonna do without a toothbrush?" I muttered.

Pendleton looked at me and grinned. "Not having a toothbrush is the least of our worries, Nick."

I knew he was right. It was a crazy thing to be upset about.

We hadn't gone more than a mile when we started running into a horde of retreating ROK soldiers coming toward us. Soon there was a steady line of ROKs on both sides of the road. But we kept going up, us in our Jeep and a single line of GIs on foot.

One line of us and two lines of ROKs!

And this was their country! It made me mad to think that they were bugging out, and we were going up to die for their land.

Klang leaned forward. "Would you look at all those sons-a-bitches."

"It makes you wonder if they're worth it, doesn't it?" I said.

Pendleton didn't say anything. But there wasn't really anything to say.

Higher up, the incline steepened. The pouring rain had turned the road into a muddy quagmire. It was heavy going, even in a Jeep. Twice we almost got bogged down.

But it was worse for the guys, on foot. They were slipping and sliding, loaded with full battle gear while the mud sucked at their boots with every step. The sloppy conditions were rapidly sapping their strength, despite the Army's attempts to get them in top physical condition and increase their endurance during basic training.

We weren't even to the top, and most of our guys were worn out. They were a rain-soaked, mud-soaked, muscle-weary bunch, with more exhaustion showing on their faces than I'd seen after a twenty-mile forced march.

A couple of them grabbed onto the side of our Jeep and hung on. But we were already in four-wheel drive and low gear, and still having trouble making it up the hill.

"You guys gotta' get off. Let go," I yelled. "We can't handle any more weight or we'll get stuck and block the road."

As tired as they were, I hated doing it, but there wasn't any choice. But I sure didn't blame them for trying.

Twenty yards farther up the road, we spotted one of our GIs, loaded down with battle gear, plus a Browning Automatic Rifle, its tripod and close to a hundred pounds of ammunition around his waist. He was struggling to make it, falling to his knees at almost every step he took.

"Look at that poor bastard, Corp," I said to Pendleton. "We're barely half-way up the mountain. He isn't going to make it."

"I see him," Pendleton replied. When we got closer, he yelled, "You, with the BAR! You can lay your weapon on our trailer and hang on the side. But nobody else."

The look of relief on that man's face was a thing to behold. "Thanks, " he said, but the shine of gratitude in his eyes spoke much louder.

After the GI succeeded in getting his weapon and gear on the trailer, Pendleton said to me and Klang "If we have to, we'll get out and push this damned Jeep, but that guy can't make it one step farther."

He didn't get any argument from either Klang or me. Maybe we couldn't help the other GIs, but we could help this one.

And if all those ROK soldiers were any indication of what was ahead of us, we were definitely going to need the BAR and ammo that GI was carrying.

Ahead of us, the road continued to snake its way up the mountain. The curtain of rain reduced visibility to only a couple hundred yards.

"Man, this rain hasn't let up one fucking bit," I grumbled.

"I thought the monsoon season was over," Klang said.

"It is,' I told him.

I remembered hearing somewhere that there were heavy rains in every war. It made me wonder if they recycled the same fucking rain.

When we finally reached the crest, we were ordered to halt. It was close to nightfall, and a command post was hurriedly set up. We were told to set up our machine gun on a high bank overlooking the road.

The ground was a mixture of reddish-brown dirt and shale-like rock that the rain quickly turned into a thick, lumpy gravy. We dug a shallow foxhole, set up our machine gun and rocket launcher, then settled down to watch and wait while the rain continued to fall.

Close to dusk, we heard sporadic gunfire coming from somewhere not far from our position. Not long afterwards, we saw a bunch of ROK soldiers coming from that same direction.

Minutes later, the distinctive rumble and clank of an approaching tank reached us. When it finally emerged from the gray rain, it was moving along the road toward us. It was the weirdest looking tank I had ever seen. The top was cut off, creating a kind of open pill box, with a machine gun mounted on it, and a cannon jutted from the front of it.

I knew right away that it wasn't an American tank, but whether it was a ROK or Chinese tank, I couldn't tell. The way the Koreans were bugging out and taking refuge behind our lines, I figured it was Korean tank, hightailing it to the rear.

It rumbled up the road, traveled past our position, and disappeared over the crest of the hill. The more I thought about that tank, the more uneasy I got. I kept remembering those GIs who had taken our command post during basic training because no one had challenged them.

I said to Pendleton, "That might have been a Chinese tank, Corp."

"Well, if it was, and it doesn't come back, then it was either Korean, or his ass has had it," he replied.

I listened for quite awhile, but I never heard any firing behind us.

After that it was quiet, but it was one miserable night we spent. We had water standing in our foxhole and more coming down. High up in the mountains the way we were, the nighttime temperature got downright chilly. I curled up in my poncho, soaked to the skin and cold to the bone. Yet I somehow managed to catch some sleep.

During the night, the rain stopped. When I woke up the next morning, my clothes were dry — from the combination of my body heat and the insulating poncho, I guess.

There was water in our canteens for drinking, but no coffee and no C rations. When we left the reserve area, there hadn't been time to grab anything more than our weapons.

It hit me that I hadn't had anything to eat since the day before. It didn't seem possible, but I wasn't even hungry. When you're scared, food is the last thing on your mind.

About an hour after daylight, a lieutenant marched up to our foxhole. "A tank came through here last night. I do not want any more coming through. Get your machine gun and set it up on the road," he ordered.

I couldn't believe what I was hearing. He wanted us to put our machine gun in the middle of the road to stop a tank! There was no machine gun made that could stop a tank. It would be suicide to try.

"But, sir, — " Pendleton tried to object.

"That is an order, Corporal. I want that machine gun on the road, and I want it there now!"

"Yes, sir." Pendleton turned to me and said, "You heard the lieutenant."

I could tell Pendleton was mad clear through, but there was no way he could disobey a direct order from a superior officer, even one as obviously green as this one was.

"I heard him," I replied.

I also knew it was an order that could get us killed. But, like the corporal, I didn't have choice but to obey. So, I moved to unlock the machine gun from its tripod.

Satisfied that his order was being carried out, the lieutenant walked off. That really ticked me. If he thought putting a machine gun on the road was so damned safe, he should have sat there beside us.

"What the hell are we going to do, Corp?" I said to Pendleton. "We can't stop a tank with this thing. They'll blow us out of the road."

"I know, but we've got our orders." Then he looked at me with a kind of smile in his eyes. "Let's just not get in a hurry about carrying them out." Turning, he said to one of our ammo bearers, "Go find a captain or some other officer from D Company and let him know what's going on here."

Off he went. In the meantime, we dawdled as much as we could, tearing down, moving and setting up the machine gun on the road. Something that should have taken only minutes, we managed to stretch out to a lot more.

But that kind of stall tactics only work for so long. When we finally used up the last one, there we were, parked in the road, praying like crazy that no enemy tanks showed up.

We stayed there, sweating it out, every minute feeling like an hour, until a captain showed up. He didn't waste any time assessing the situation — or any words.

"Get your asses off this fucking road right now! Who's the idiot that ordered this?"

With considerable satisfaction, we fingered the lieutenant responsible, then tore that machine gun down and moved off that road faster than we'd ever done it in our lives.

As for the captain, he tracked down that lieutenant and chewed him up one side and down the other. His voice must have carried for miles.

"What in hell were you thinking? We've got enough casualties without you killing these men off! You're an infantry lieutenant. You should know that a man with a .30 caliber machine gun can't stop a tank."

That captain had a lot more to say, and we enjoyed every word of it, although we were careful not to laugh too loudly.

Pendleton summed up our feelings when he said, "The son-of-a-bitch had it coming."

Instead of going back to our foxhole along the bank by the road, we were ordered to take up a position on the other side of the road farther along the hill.

We hadn't been there very long when two ROK soldiers came up, carrying an air-cooled machine gun and some ammunition. Right away they started setting up their gun right beside ours.

As soon as I realized what they were doing, I yelled, "Hey, you guys get out of here!"

Placing two machine guns side by side is just about the worst mistake that can be made in combat.

But those two ROKs didn't seem to understand. "Americans. Americans," they said, which was probably all the English they knew.

Since we couldn't make them leave, we moved to another location that gave us a good vantage point over the road below.

"Man, that was stupid," I said to Pendleton. "Don't they know you're never supposed to do that."

"They're probably scared, especially after all their comrades bugged out on them. At least those two are staying and trying to make a fight of it. You have to give them credit for that."

I agreed.

Late that afternoon, we received orders to move again, this time to an abandoned machine gun bunker near the top of the hill. On our way to the new location, we passed some ROK soldiers lying dead on the road. It looked like they had been there for awhile. We didn't have any choice but to leave them where they were.

As soon as we reached the bunker, we set up our machine gun on the dirt table inside. We noticed how slippery the surface of the table and bunker floor felt, but it wasn't until morning that we discovered the bunker's previous occupants had crapped all over it, and we had been stepping in the stuff all night long.

Dickerson, our new platoon sergeant showed up the next morning with new orders. We were moving out yet again. Believe me, we were damned glad to leave that bunker and its smelly crap.

Loaded down with our machine gun and ammo, we joined the rest of our rifle company at the assembly point. This time, we didn't have a Jeep and trailer waiting to transport us or our gear. Just like all the other soldiers, we were traveling on foot.

We headed down the hill and onto the dirt road. Near the bottom, some ROK soldiers opened fire on us. We scrambled for cover, not sure whether we should return fire. After all, they were supposed to be on our side.

But one of the officers quickly set us straight on that. "If you're fired upon, you fire back."

So we opened up. The shooting stopped shortly after that. I don't know whether we actually hit any of the ROKs, or if they simply realized their mistake and quit shooting.

We moved back onto the road and followed it all the way down to the floor of a narrow valley. A stream cut through the length of it, its waters still running brown with the runoff from the heavy rains.

Farther down, a second road came out of the hills on the opposite side of the valley, crossed a bridge over the stream, and intersected the road we were on.

Our road snaked along the base of the hills, curving in and out below a taller hill we called Five Fingers because of the ridged slopes that jutted into the valley floor from it.

As we were traveling along it, I heard the distinctive whine of artillery shells. Before the first shell exploded, there was yelling up and down our line.

"Incoming! Take cover! Take cover!"

By then I had already spotted a small, hollowed-out area, notched into the hillside close to me. As I dived for it, so did Pendleton and Joe, the assistant gunner. All three of us piled into the same small space like a trio of ostriches feeling safe because our heads were covered.

All around us guys scattered to get off the road as round after round slammed into it with a series of thundering booms. Some of the guys sought shelter along the hillside, but most of them headed into an open stretch of flat ground between the road and the stream.

In seconds there were more explosions and screams mixing in with the thunder of the artillery shells. At first I thought a shell had taken out some of our guys. I snuck a look between explosions and saw more than half of our guys lying in that open field. The rest of them were scurrying to get out of it instead of taking cover.

Not understanding, I started to say, "What the hell's going — "

Just about then the ground erupted under one of our guys, sending him flying into a heap.

"Sweet Jesus, it's a mine field," Pendleton murmured beside me.

I watched in horror as more of our guys tripped more mines, even the ones who had been carefully trying to retrace their steps to the road.

What was worse — not all of them were killed instantly. The few who were wounded and still conscious called out for help. Listening to their cries tore my guts out. Those guys were my buddies.

"There must be something we can do," I murmured. But I knew there wasn't — not with the ongoing artillery barrage.

Even without it, entering that minefield would be a slow, inch-by-inch process. You've seen it in the movies — a guy probing the ground with a knife to locate a mine, then carefully defusing it. Such a rescue would take hours, and couldn't even be attempted as long as the enemy was active in the area.

"There's nothing we can do, Nick," Pendleton said. "And it sure as hell isn't safe anywhere along this road. We've gotta get outta here. Come on."

With the Chinese artillery zeroed on the road and the mine field on the valley side of it, there seemed to be only one safe direction, and that was up.

We scrambled up the brush-covered slope to escape the barrage. For awhile, little bunches of our outfit were scattered all over the top of Five Fingers, with nobody knowing where anybody else was. Once we finally made contact, we regrouped and started digging foxholes.

As soon as we had ours dug, we mounted our machine gun and settled down to wait. From our position, I had a clear view of the roads and the bridge in the valley below — and the minefield where our guys lay dead or dying.

The minefield wasn't shown on any of our maps. We didn't know if the ROKs had planted the mines and failed to notify the U.N. Forces or if it was the work of the Chinese. Whatever the case, it had wiped out over half of our company.

Every now and then, I thought I saw one of them move. I wondered if it was our platoon sergeant and knew there couldn't be a worse way to die. I thanked God it wasn't me lying down there, and I thanked Him, too, that I was too far away to hear their moans for help. The memory of them echoed in my mind just the same.

Farther down the valley, I noticed a large stack of artillery rounds stockpiled at the base of the opposite hill. It was the ammunitions supply of our Triple Nickel Artillery that had been overrun by the Chinese.

A half dozen Red Chinese were scurrying around, carting off the ammo a shell at a time, and taking them back into the hills on the other side of the valley.

I turned to one of the guys from the rifle company and said, "See if you can pick any of those Chinks off."

He hesitated, then shook his head. "I can't do that."

I knew right away that he was another green replacement who had never been in combat, never fired his weapon at anything other than a target. It went against everything the poor bastard knew to shoot at someone who wasn't already shooting at him.

But those were our guys laying out there in that mine field. Maybe there hadn't been anything I could do to help Sergeant Dickerson or the rest of them, but there sure as hell was something I could do to keep those bastards over there from killing any more of us.

"Give me that rifle." I took the M-1 from him and started taking potshots at them.

I wasn't sure but I thought I hit a couple of them. Then I noticed a soldier close to the bridge. His uniform didn't look like anything I'd seen a ROK soldier wearing. Zeroing in on him, I squeezed off another shot and nailed him.

The kid beside me protested, "He could have been a ROK."

I just looked at him. "So?"

I knew it could have been a straggler from the ROK division that the Chinese had overrun. But I didn't really give a damn, not when I remembered the way they had bugged out — two lines of them heading to the rear while one line of our guys advanced to plug the gap they had left in our lines.

It wasn't long before one of our tanks clattered into view on the road below. Halting, it swiveled its .50 caliber machine gun toward the ammo dump and fired rounds at it, clearly intent on blowing up the ammunition to keep the enemy from making off with any more of it.

When the tank's first round hit its target, I expected the whole thing to go up in a huge ball of flame — like in the movies. But that's another one of those myths created by Hollywood's special effects. It doesn't happen that way in real life.

That tank fired round after round at that ammo dump, destroying little pieces of it at a time, with ordinary, everyday pop-pop-pop explosions.

One of the guys in the tank spotted our machine gun nest on the hillside and hollered up, "Hey! We're short a gunner! Have you got anybody you can spare to man our machine gun?"

"Sorry, no can do," Pendleton yelled back.

Being a gunner on a tank was a job none of us wanted. Tanks are the first target an enemy wants to take out. On a tank, you're practically asking to get hit.

It didn't take long for the Chinese artillery to retaliate for the attack on the ammo dump and open fire. That tank wisely got the hell out of there.

But the Chinese weren't satisfied with just driving the tank off. They switched their focus to the hill where we were. With shells pounding down all around our position, I hunkered down in our foxhole and wished for the hundredth time that I had a flak jacket.

Seven

The shelling continued off and on throughout the day. After being on Outposts Tom and Harry, I was sure that could mean only one thing — somewhere close by the Chinese were massing for an attack and advancing under the cover of the artillery barrage. And with so many of our guys lying in that minefield, I also knew we weren't up to strength.

Off to our left, I started hearing the rapid chatter of exchanging gunfire. It came from the hill area held by the ROK Marine division. A red flare went up, arcing across the sky like a Communist sickle. It was the signal for the assault by the Chinese on those ROK Marines.

A daylight attack by the Chinese — that was something new in my experience. And it made me all the more edgy as I sat there in the foxhole, watching the steep slope below our machine gun position. There was no movement anywhere along it.

We waited, listening to the sounds of intense fighting the hot summer wind carried to us. I knew that ROK Marine division was really catching hell. I also knew if they didn't hold their position, we would be outflanked, just like the Chinese had briefly succeeded in doing to us on Outpost Harry.

I doubted that possibility had crossed the minds of any of new replacements with us, but I suspected Corporal Pendleton had thought about it. He looked as tense and alert as I was.

From our position, I couldn't see any of the fighting, only hear it. I listened for any subtle shift in its sound that might tell me which side was winning.

At some point I caught the sound of voices coming from the slope below us, talking in that gobble-de-gook that could have been either Korean or Chinese.

"Corp," I said.

Pendleton nodded. "I hear 'em."

As I scanned the scarred slope, trying to locate them, two soldiers ambled into view, chatting between themselves. They looked like ROK soldiers, but I wasn't sure.

They made their way toward our position on a shoulder of the hill, casual as you please. I figured them for a pair of ROK stragglers, but the back of my neck kept prickling with suspicion.

My mind kept flashing back to those two GIs who had fooled me back in basic training - and to the time when I'd been distracted on Outpost Tom by those two Chinese jabbering away in the dark, smoking cigarettes.

Just in case, I kept one eye on the ROKs and one eye on the rest of the hill to make sure there weren't any Chinese sneaking up while we were preoccupied by the two men in plain view.

When the two soldiers crested the shoulder of that hill, I got my first clear look at their weapons.

"Burp gun!" I yelled, at roughly the same time somebody else hollered the warning.

Just that quick, the two soldiers swung their rifles up and opened fire. In the same second, Pendleton hit the machine gun and I started firing along with a dozen or so others. A bullet sang past my head just before the two Chinese twisted to the ground, shot to pieces.

Luck was with us this time; none of our guys were hit.

One of the officers went through the pockets of the two Chinese and took what papers he found, then ordered a couple of privates to bury them.

That was more than we could do for our own guys, still laying out there in the mine field, their bodies already bloating in the one hundred-plus degree temperature of full sun.

All night long we listened to the sounds of the battle being waged, hearing the ebb and flow of it. First, the Chinese pushed the ROKs back; then the counterattack by the ROKs pushed the Chinese back. The night was alive with signaling flares and the tootling of Chinese buglers.

Through it all, the Chinese kept up their barrage on our position, pinning us down and keeping us out of the fight.

And I kept praying those ROK Marines would hold the line against the Chinese. I knew if they failed, our flank would be exposed and we would be facing the enemy on two sides. Knowing that fills you with a tension that is as sharp as a barber's razor.

It was clear those ROK Marines were putting up a helluva fight. I was just glad it was them and not us.

Come daylight, the ROK Marines still held the hill. But none of us thought, not even for a minute, that the fighting was over.

The latest scuttlebutt claimed that the Chinese were determined to seize more territory and improve their position before signing any peace agreement in Panmunjom. Considering the success they'd already had, breaking through our lines, they weren't about to quit yet.

Which meant I was stuck in this foxhole, trying to plug the gap with all the others and baking under the glare of a hot, July sun. By now, our canteens were almost empty, and we are sitting there sweating up a storm. We're all trying to save what little water we had left, but thirst was starting to get to us.

My mouth was so dry that I couldn't even lick my lips and get any moisture. To add to the torture, there was the stream right below us. Every now and then, I would hear the cool sound of running water. It only made me thirstier.

Somebody suggested, "Try sucking on a rock. It helps."

It sounded like the kind of advice you would hear in a Hollywood movie, and I didn't put much stock in them anymore. But I tried it anyway. The darn thing worked. I was actually able to work up a little moisture in my mouth. That provided some relief, but not much.

But in the blistering summer heat, with little or no shade, water was a critical need. One of the guys in the rifle company located a small stream on the back side of the hill. Even though there was a dead Chinese lying in it and we had no pills to purify it, it was water.

We knew it was likely contaminated with God-knows-what, but most of us figured it was worth the risk and filled our canteens. We were careful, though, not to drink too much of it.

With the Chinese artillery still commanding all the approaches to our position, the Army hadn't been able to get any supplies to us. That meant we were still without food.

By then I had lost count of how many days it had been since I ate last. I knew my stomach should have been gnawing on my backbone, but for some strange reason, I wasn't one hungry. But our lack of good water and a re-supply of ammunition — now, that worried me.

I didn't have as much to worry about as I thought. Later that afternoon, word flashed across the hill that a bunch of gutsy guys from the motor pool had torn down the road like a bat out of hell and dropped off supplies and ammunition as well as fresh replacements for us. A supply dump of sorts had been set up in an area some distance to the rear of our point position on the hill.

For some reason, I got designated to be the one to get supplies for our machine crew. I jogged to the top of the hill and worked my around to a side slope that overlooked the road. A short distance below was the mine field. There, a bunker-like storage area had been dug into the side of the hill to hold the new supplies. I loaded myself down with as much as I could carry and trotted back to our machine gun nest.

I swear, C-rations had never tasted so good to me as they from did when I took the first bite from that cold can of corned beef hash. But after nearly three days without food, I was careful not to eat too much. I didn't want to make myself sick.

Word soon came down with the welcome news that replacements had arrive to relieve us on the point. We would be shifted back to a support position elsewhere on the hill. As soon as darkness fell, we received our orders to move out.

It was a bright, moonlit night. The sky was scattered with stars, and the hill became a patchwork of deep shadows and moon-silvered ground. The visibility couldn't have been better for a night move.

As always, the rifle company led the way. Pendleton, Joe the assistant gunner, Klang, myself, and a ROK soldier who had attached himself to our machine gun crew, brought up the rear.

Once we reached the hilltop, we traveled along it for a distance, then dipped into a long ravine that stretched all the way down to the valley. A little way up the other side of it, we came to an old trench about two-and-a-half to three feet deep.

The leader of the rifle company called a halt there, deciding that we would take a short break before continuing to our new support position. It was quiet, almost peaceful, and we were moving in the right direction — away from the Chinese front.

But as safe as it seemed, old habits are hard to break for any combat veteran.

Purely out of habit and ingrained training, we went ahead and set up the machine gun on the trench bank. After we locked it on its tripod, we fed a belt of ammunition into it and clicked in a round, even though we were only stopping for a short, ten-minute break.

After we were set up, I settled against the trench wall between Pendleton and Klang, my rifle laying across my lap, and thought about lighting up a cigarette.

Suddenly there was some movement in the area we had just crossed. I looked and saw two pale figures in the moonlight, moving in that all-too-familiar hunched-over posture, as they jumped the trench.

At the same instant, Pendleton yelled, "Chinese!"

The second he shouted the warning, alarm shot through me — so strong, it was close to panic. Then, it hit me that we had the damned machine gun pointed in the wrong direction. And the rifle company, instead of being between us and the enemy, they were behind us! There wasn't anything could do about the rifle company, but the machine gun was a different story.

Pendleton was already a split second ahead of me. All in one motion, it seemed, he released the machine gun from the tripod, picked it up and swung it around, anchoring it between his knees. The muzzle of it was level with my left ear when he rattled off the long burst, the flashes from them burning the side of my face.

But I was too busy shooting at any sign of movement to be conscious of more than the sensation of heat against my cheek and the racket of it in my ears.

Joe, the assistant gunner, threw himself onto the trench floor next to Pendleton and grabbed the ammunition belt to keep feeding bullets into the chamber. In front of me, Klang fired off a couple shots at something. The ROK soldier didn't do anything.

All the time my mind was racing right along with my heart — Where had those Chinese come from? How many were out there? Was it a small patrol or a larger force? If it was larger, what the hell were we gonna do?

Even as I was firing, I was silently praying, 'Sweet Jesus, do I ever need your help. Please, God. Please.'

The moonlight briefly glinted on something pale — an arm, maybe. Then a stick grenade exploded close by. Then another, and another.

BOOM! BOOM! BOOM!

Grenades erupted all around us, close enough to throw dirt and debris into the trench.

We all opened fire, spraying bullets over the trench and ravine area in an effort to drive the Chinese back out of grenade range. I saw one Chinese rise up, get hit and fall backwards.

But the minute we let up firing, more grenades landed. Each one seemed to explode a little bit closer than the last.

The action became a blur of red tracer bullets streaking through the night and vague shapes moving in the shadows, ducking here, jumping the trench there. The almost constant chat-chat-chatter of the machine gun hammered against my ears. The rifle kicked again and again against my shoulder as the ground erupted with the explosion of another grenade. Fear turned into a kind of blind rage to get the bastards before they got me.

I didn't know how many were out there, but it looked like a bunch. And all of them seemed to be intent on taking out the machine gun. A machine gun position was always a prime target in any enemy infantry attack.

I was scared, praying, cursing and firing all at the same time. Suddenly my gun jammed. I reached around and snatched the rifle the ROK had. He sure as hell wasn't making use of it.

Seconds later there was a lull in the fighting. I offered up a silent prayer that the Chinese were retreating, but I had the uneasy feeling they were regrouping to hit us again.

My ears rang from the concussions of the machine gun blasts that had also burned my cheek. There was blood coming from my nose and ears. I wiped the worst of it on my sleeve.

Pendleton's legs were burned by the machine gun's hot shell casings landing on them. Other than that, all four of us had come through relatively unscathed. I knew we had been damned lucky, considering none of us had on flak jackets.

But there we were, lined up in the trench like a row of sitting ducks. One burst from a Chinese burp gun would wipe us all out. Knowing that sent a cold chill down my spine. So far, the Chinese had relied on grenades. I just prayed that their accuracy didn't improve.

I looked around. "Where the hell is our rifle company?"

In all the confusion, I couldn't remember hearing any supporting fire coming from them.

"I don't know." Pendleton glanced up the trench.

There was the rifle company, a good twenty-five yards farther up the trench. Instead of coming to our defense, they had moved back, too far to give us any protection.

We were on our own. Four against who knew how many? I didn't count the ROK soldier because he wasn't doing anything but cowering in the trench. I thanked God that we were all still alive. I also knew a lot of that was due to Pendleton's quick action bringing the machine gun into play.

Recognizing that, I said to Pendleton, "I'm going to put you in for a medal on this, Corp."

"I would like that very much, Nick," he replied in a quiet and steady voice.

Just then, another grenade exploded as the Chinese came at us again, still relying on grenades. We opened fire, the machine gun once more blasting next to my ears. And I kept praying that God would interfere with their accuracy.

In the back of my mind, I kept remembering something I'd been told in basic training — according to statistics, a machine gun position is usually wiped out after roughly an hour of fighting. But I had no idea how much time had passed since we spotted that first Chinese, five minutes or fifty.

But I did know that without support from our rifle company, we were in deep trouble.

There was another break in the action. Suddenly, at the top of the slope ten feet above our position, a soldier popped up, silhouetted against moonlit sky. Klang swung his rifle up, but didn't fire.

Aware that he'd never been in combat before, I turned and fired. But I shot too quickly and missed. In that instant, I knew I was dead. I could literally feel the bullet slamming into me. I could feel myself dying.

The soldier on hilltop yelled, "GI! GI!"

With a shock, I realized he was one of our guys. I wasn't dead after all.

Furious, Pendleton shouted up, "What the hell are you doing?! Either hit the deck or get down here. One or the other!"

The guy disappeared.

I barely had time to register the fact that GIs were on the hill above us before the Chinese came again, throwing more grenades. This time they exploded much closer, shaking the ground beneath us and pelting us with dirt and debris.

There were too many of them, too close; I knew that even as we all kept firing. I had a split-second's glimpse of a grenade bouncing into the trench. I don't know how, but Pendleton managed to scoop it up and throw it out, saving all of us.

But it was only a matter of time.

In the next breath, it seemed, an explosion rocked the ground under me. Joe was dead; Pendleton was wounded, and the machine gun was damaged beyond use. By some miracle, neither Klang nor I were hurt.

Grabbing my shoulder, Pendleton gave me a shove out of the trench and yelled something. But there was so much roaring in my ears from the machine gun racket that I couldn't hear what he said. When I signaled that to him, he motioned for us to go. Then he picked up a carbine and started shooting at the Chinese. I never heard a single shot but I saw the muzzle flash.

When he motioned for us to leave a second time, I realized he was ordering Klang and me to get the hell out of there while he covered our retreat.

Without the machine gun, I knew we were all goners. I yelled at Klang, "Come on!" and started scrambling up the slope to the hilltop. I knew there were GIs up there. And I wanted to get the hell out of that trench. Klang was right on my heels.

Just as we hauled ourselves over the crest, I felt the ground tremble with the impact of another explosion. I looked back. There was nothing moving in the trench except smoke and dust. I knew Pendleton had gotten it. We never had a chance to cover his retreat.

He had died saving our lives. And probably the lives of those in the rifle company as well as the poor, dumb GIs on the hill.

We weren't out of danger yet, though — not with all those Chinese down below. But there was a definite sense of weight knowing that Pendleton was dead and I was alive. It was part guilt and part a feeling of obligation that is difficult to explain. I owed him a debt I couldn't repay — except, maybe, by staying alive.

Knowing there wasn't anything more we could do for Pendelton, Klang and I moved away from the crest and met up with the GIs already there. A couple machine gunners from our Dog Company recognized us and motioned for us to join them.

With the moon shining almost as bright as day, we dug in and waited, anticipating an attack by the Chinese from the ravine. We waited, but they never came.

To this day, I don't know if the Chinese retreated after their planned attack was thwarted by our accidental discovery of them, or if they hit somewhere else and were thrown back. I was so deafened by the machine gun blasts and grenade explosions that I couldn't hear whether there was any firing going on elsewhere in our area.

The guys had to literally shout in my ear for me to hear anything. Even then it sounded like a tiny voice coming from miles and miles away.

First thing the next morning, the guys on the machine gun told me that they needed the spare parts box Klang and I had left in the trench when we made our escape from it. I didn't want to go back down there, not with Pendleton and Joe still lying in the trench.

But those spare parts were needed to repair their machine guns, and those repairs could be critical if the Chinese decided to attack our position. Since I knew where we'd left the box, I was the logical one to go get it.

Everything inside me was screaming, knotting my muscles up so much that I couldn't even make myself look at Pendleton when I got there. I just grabbed the spare parts box and got the hell out of the trench and back on the hilltop.

A detail went out later to bring back the bodies of Pendleton and the assistant gunner, and search the bodies of the Chinese that we had killed.

From one of them, Sergeant Day brought back a letter and some family photos. The Chinese were people with loved ones back home just like us. Back then, I didn't care. They had killed my corporal and I hated them.

The dead Chinese were hurriedly buried in shallow graves. One of the graves was so shallow that a foot of its corpse stuck out. When I saw it poking out of the ground, I opened up with the machine gun and shot it full of holes. That's how strong my hatred was at that moment.

At some point I was told fifteen Chinese had been killed during the firefight and the Army estimated we may have faced as many as two enemy companies. Myself, I have no idea how many Chinese were out there that night. I only remember seeing maybe a dozen, although there easily could have been many more under cover elsewhere along the ravine. It's for sure that we surprised them before they had a chance to attack any of our positions.

But we couldn't be certain that the Chinese wouldn't be return to try again.

Eight

The next couple days are blurred in my mind. Maybe because I couldn't hear. Or maybe because, by then, my nerves were pretty well shattered.

If you talked to others, they would probably tell you that I had what we called back then — the thousand yard stare. You're there, but you're not there. You can act and react, but it's almost robot-like.

I could still function as a soldier, deaf or not, a little crazy or not, and that's all that was important with the enemy active in the area.

Pendleton's death meant that I was now the ranking member of our gun crew. Sergeant Day, the platoon sergeant gave me a machine gun and an assistant gunner. But, as usual, we were so short of men that my assistant was a second lieutenant.

While the lieutenant and I were making our way to the bunker we'd been assigned to, the Chinese artillery started shelling our position. Since I couldn't hear the incoming shells, the lieutenant worked out signals with me — one hit on the helmet meant 'take cover', and two hits was the 'all clear' signal.

After a couple days, I got some of my hearing back, but my nerves were still pretty fired. I can remember sitting at my machine gun, holding a hand grenade with my finger in the pin, ready to pull it. I was so wired that I was bouncing up and down the whole time, unable to stop, and not really even aware of what I was doing.

The lieutenant took one look at me and said, "Give me that hand grenade."

I refused, insisting, "I'm all right."

"No, you're not. Now give me that grenade."

When I ignored him, he took it from me.

Like I said, my nerves were pretty well shot.

Sergeant Day later told me that they had tried to get me off the hill, but they needed every able-bodied man they had. While it was true I couldn't hear and I was close too being a basket case, I could still shoot. And that's all the Army was interested in.

The situation along the line didn't change a whole lot over the next five days, except that I began to hear a little better. However, I continued to have that high-pitched ringing in my ears. The volume of it was about the level of the loudest siren you can imagine. It wasn't something I felt right complaining about, considering Pendleton had gotten killed and all I suffered was a loss of hearing. The thought of Pendleton was always with me, mostly in the back of my mind, but never far from the front.

About five days later we were reinforced by a handful of replacements. By then, it had been ten days since I'd had a bath, a shave or a change of clothes. We all probably stunk to high heaven, but we were all so used to the smell that we didn't notice it anymore.

As for my clothes, that was a different matter. They were so stiff with dirt and dried sweat, they could have walked around by themselves.

Then, the reinforcements arrived, complete with a change of clothes. The minute I saw that, I turned to one of them who was about my size and said, "Can I have the fatigues you're wearing?"

"What?" He stared at me like I had lost my mind. I probably looked that way, too, — all filthy and wild with a thick, black beard and scraggly hair.

"I've been wearing these same clothes for ten days," I told him. "You may think those fatigues of yours are dirty, but to me, they look clean."

Right about then, I wasn't sure if I remembered what clean felt like.

The guy hesitated, then felt sorry for me, and agreed. "Take them."

I grabbed up those fatigues and stripped down to my dirty underwear right there on the spot. When I put on those clothes of his, I swear I actually felt clean for the first time in days. I don't think that GI ever understood how thankful I was to have them.

* * *

On the Twenty-fourth of July, word filtered down that the Greek Battalion had arrived at the command post to relieve us. Somebody

80

decided that I was the one most familiar with the terrain between our position and the command post. Therefore I was tagged to be the one to go back and bring them up that night.

After dark, I made my way back to the CP and hooked up with the Greek outfit. The minute they saw my black beard and eyes, they mistook me for one of them and started jabbering away in their own language.

"Wait a minute," I said. "Doesn't anybody here speak English?"

One of them stepped forward. "I do."

He identified himself as an officer, but there was nothing on his uniform that indicated his rank. When I asked him about it, he explained that, in combat situations, Greek officers button a flap over their rank to prevent the enemy from targeting them. He assured me that the Greek soldiers knew exactly which ones were their officers.

We left the command area and headed up the hill toward our position. It was a hefty climb. At roughly the halfway point, we reached a low hollow just below the crest and stopped there to take a break.

Right away all these Greek soldiers started lighting up cigarettes. I nearly panicked when I saw that. Here we were, essentially on the front lines, within shouting distance of the Chinese who had been shelling the hell out of us for ten days and these fools were lighting cigarettes, revealing our location to the enemy.

"No! No!" I shouted and waved my hands. "Put those out! Put those out!"

Naturally they couldn't understand me. So I turned to their commanding officer. "Tell them to put those cigarettes out. The Chinese have been shelling the piss out of us. As soon as one of their spotters sees the glow of those cigarettes, we'll be dead ducks."

He snapped out an order, and the red dots of all those burning cigarette tips winked out.

But it shook the hell out of me. I didn't draw an easy breath until we started out again. And I made sure there weren't any more rest stops along the way.

Once the Greeks had taken over our positions, we moved about mile to the rear. And I was thankful that if the Chinese artillery opened up, this time it was the Greeks who would get shelled instead of us.

After a day and a half of rest, uninterrupted by enemy artillery, we were ordered to go back on line July Twenty-sixth. As the highest ranking survivor from our machine gun crew, I was assigned my own ammo bearers and assistant gunner. This time our machine gun bunker was high on the hillside overlooking the ammo dump and the road and unmarked minefield below it.

It was a sad spot. The bodies of our guys were still out in that minefield. After days of lying in the hot July sun, the corpses were bloated beyond recognition. Many of them had exploded in the heat. And that damnable Korean wind blew the smell from them all over us. Sometimes it was so potent, I almost gagged from it.

Over and over again, I wished there had been some way to get their bodies out of there before now. But I knew there hadn't been, not with all the shelling and enemy patrols in the area these last twelve days.

On the afternoon of July 27, 1953, we received word that a cease-fire was supposed to take effect at ten o'clock that night. I was half afraid to believe it would actually come about. I'd been on this death row they called the combat zone for so long that it was like having a pardon dangled in front of me. I wanted to grab it, but I was also worried that at the last second it would get jerked out of my reach. And the Chinese had never given me any reason to trust them.

But, peace. Dear God, how I wanted it all to end.

As sun sank that night, there was a different kind of tension in the air. Somewhere between eight and nine o'clock, I heard the spiraling whine of artillery shells. At first I thought it was outgoing mail, fired by our artillery. But the Chinese had targeted one of our rear areas for bombardment. The shells were flying so high over our heads, they sounded like out-going.

I didn't particularly care where they were going. I was just damned glad they weren't landing on us.

It wasn't long before our artillery opened up. Soon the skyline behind us was one long and giant, crimson glow. The air rumbled with the thunder of the distant explosions. There was no let up in any of it as the minutes crept closer and closer to ten o clock.

While I was glad we weren't getting shelled, the endless bombardment also made me nervous. I'd been in enough combat situations to know that using an artillery barrage to cover troop advancement was one of the enemy's favorite tactics. For all I knew, this cease-fire could be another one of their tricks to take us by surprise.

But there was also the chance it might not be a trick. I clung to that thought, hoping against hope that this cease-fire would be the real thing.

We had orders to clear our weapons at precisely fifteen minutes before ten, but to keep the ammunition close at hand. None of the guys in my machine gun crew had seen any combat before. As soon as I got the machine gun cleared, I checked each and every one of their weapons to make sure they were unloaded.

If anything went wrong with this cease-fire I didn't want it to be because one of my guys fired first, accidentally or otherwise.

At a quarter 'til ten, our weapons were empty, but those Chinese artillery rounds continued to sail over our heads, and a steady roll of thunder continued to come from our rear.

All we could do was sweat it out. And this is one time when that phrase describes the situation perfectly.

Suddenly, at ten minutes before ten, there was absolute silence. There wasn't a sound anywhere. The Chinese had stopped firing, and it was so quiet it was downright scary.

The official hour of the cease-fire came. Still nothing. Just empty silence.

All that night, we waited and watched, on one-hundred per cent alert, searching the shadows for those humped shapes of Chinese soldiers stealing toward our position. Nothing. It was beginning to look like this cease-fire was really going to hold.

Morning came, and the wind died. The sun rose to throw its full light on the valley below us. From our machine gun position, we had a clear view of the dirt road that wound along the base of the hill, the minefields and the stream beyond it.

My heart skipped about ten beats when I suddenly saw this parade of Chinese soldiers coming along the road. Worse yet, some of them were driving our Jeeps and pulling the 105s they'd seized when they over-ran our Triple Nickel Artillery.

They marched along the road directly below us, as bold as you please. A few of them broke away from the column and darted to the base of the hill, laying down what looked like gifts of food and silk scarves.

I didn't know what the hell was going on. Maybe they were just as glad as we were that the fighting was over. And maybe they were deliberately taunting us, trying to get us to fire the first shot and break the truce.

Our weapons were still cleared. But all that meant was that we didn't have a live round in the firing chamber. Believe me, you can click one in damned fast. I knew that, and I knew these green recruits in my gun crew were a little scared.

I turned to them and said, "If any of you sons-a-bitches even get near that machine gun, I'll shoot you myself. Unless they fire on us, we aren't gonna' be the ones to start this war again."

They got the message. But I wasn't feeling any easier. I kept remembering those two Chinese smoking a cigarette on Outpost Tom, and those other two walking up this very hill, chattering away. This could be just another attempt by the Chinese to occupy our attention while another bunch snuck up on us.

That's what combat does to you. It makes you suspicious of anything and everything.

I told my men to keep their eyes sharp and make sure none of those bastards were creeping up the hillside somewhere else.

"Why? There's a cease fire," one of them argued.

"Maybe. But I experienced a diversion like this before, and it almost got me killed."

But this time it was only a parade. Maybe it was a friendly one, but for me, it was nerve-wracking. After awhile, the Chinese marched back behind their own lines. All was quiet again.

And it stayed that way.

Finally, on the 31st of July, we were relieved and ordered four miles to the rear. We started down the hill, carrying our machine guns and ammunition, grenades hooked to our belts.

We'd been two weeks living mostly on nerve. Now the adrenaline was gone and exhaustion had set in. The weight of the guns, ammo and grenades became too much, and we dumped it all in a field because we were all too damned tired to carry it one step farther.

We were still dragging when we came to some MPs on the road. The MPs weren't exactly happy with the slowness of our pace, and they were damned quick to tell us about it.

"Hey, you guys, move the hell out! Get your fat asses going and step it up! Move it! Move it! Move it!"

Talk like that might buffalo a green recruit, but it didn't carry any weight with the combat-wise in our group, especially when it came on the same road where some of our buddies got killed.

I just looked at them and said, "Where the hell were you when we were getting our asses shot off?"

Somebody else challenged, "You weren't pushing the enemy around, were you?"

The minute those MPs saw how hostile we were, they changed their tune. "Sorry, but we've got to keep you moving and get everybody back."

I knew that was their job. I had no problem with that, only with their attitude.

When we reached the rear area, the Army had a hot meal waiting for us — our first in two weeks. I was almost too tired to eat mine.

But I ran into Kinnaman, my sister's brother-in-law. I had lost track of him when we were all rushed forward to fill the gap. I didn't know where he had ended up, but I knew he had to have seen some action. Everybody did.

"Well, Kinnaman," I said, recalling how gung-ho he had been to get into battle. "Have you had enough of combat?"

He smiled a little smile that held a world of understanding, and replied, "I came over here to fight, Nick. But I'm gonna' see if I can't get in the motor pool and drive Jeeps for awhile."

Eventually that's what he did. And I didn't blame him either. Very few guys who have been in combat ever want to experience it again. Afterwards, it's like that line in that old gospel song "I ain't gonna' study war no more."

Once we got back in blocking, the Army decided it was time we looked like soldiers again, and we all had to shave.

Now, my whiskers have always been the fast-growing kind. By late afternoon, I usually have a very dark five o'clock shadow. It's nothing for me to shave twice a day.

After two weeks without a razor, I had a full-grown beard. Plus, the left side of my face was still raw from the powder burns I got from the machine gun blasts. I wasn't eager to run a razor blade over it.

So I asked one of the officers, "Can we grow sideburns?"

He seemed a little surprised by my question, thought about it a second, then said, "Why, yes, you can."

"How long can they be?"

"I don't think it makes much difference," he replied.

With Kinnaman acting as my barber, we went to work on my beard, first with scissors, then a razor. It was slow going because we didn't have any soap to soften my whiskers, only water.

Kinnaman went through three razors by the time he finally got down to my skin, but he was careful to avoid the burned area on my cheek. When he finished, I had sideburns that resembled mutton chops.

Never once did I forget my promise to Pendleton, or the debt I owed him.

The next day Klang and I looked up the First sergeant of our Dog Company and informed him of Pendleton's death and the circumstances surrounding it. I told the First Sergeant that I thought Pendleton should get a medal, just like I promised him I would. Klang said the same thing. The sergeant agreed and mentioned something about putting us all in for a bronze medal.

Afterwards I felt a little better, knowing that I had kept my word to Pendleton. He had saved a lot of lives that night, not just mine, — maybe even more than we knew at the time. His sacrifice definitely deserved to be recognized.

Looking back, I know I should have reported for sick call at that time. But I figured that the burns on my face were starting to heal and I had already gotten some of my hearing back, although it still wasn't good. But because it had gradually begun to return, I decided that, in time, the rest of it would come back and the roaring in my ears would go away, too. Besides, I was raised to believe that a man doesn't complain about something so minor as this.

After five days, with the cease-fire still holding, we moved another three miles to the rear and assumed a blocking position. We were back in the Army's version of civilization, with tents, cots, hot showers, movies, and beer.

Our mail caught up with us, as well. Lo and behold, what did we find in that first batch, but autographed photos from Debbie Reynolds! Talk about a high point after the hell we'd just come through, that was it.

The letter we had sent her, addressed simply to Debbie Reynolds, Hollywood, California, had not only reached her, but she had answered it, too — in less than two months! That was a morale boost to end all morale boosts.

* * *

Not long after we arrived in blocking, Blackburn rejoined us. I was never so glad to see anybody. In a way, it was like having my brother come back.

Blackburn looked around at all the new faces and said, "Where is everybody?"

I told him about Pendleton being killed, as well as about the sergeant and the other guys in our rifle company walking into an unmarked minefield.

For a minute he didn't say anything, then just shook his head. "I knew you guys were going into hell when the Chinese broke through the ROK lines. I tried to get transferred back so I could join you, but my request was turned down. I feel bad that I wasn't there with you."

I knew Blackburn meant every word of it. In combat, you don't fight for a bunch of high ideals; you fight for your buddies as well as to save your own neck. That's all you're thinking about. That's what Pendleton was thinking about when he sprang into action that night. Plus, he was our corporal. I know that must have increased his feeling of responsibility. His death wasn't something I would ever forget.

"I'm glad you weren't there," I told Blackburn. "It wasn't good."

Blackburn knew the talk was getting heavy, and tried to lighten it. "That sergeant owed me a lot of money."

"Well," I said. "His debt is cleared now."

Nine

During those first three or four weeks after we came off line, things were quiet. An area called the Demilitarized Zone had been established along the former front lines. Instead of combat, we were now on guard duty.

Like everybody else, I did my hitch on the DMZ, manning a machine gun and watching to make sure no North Korean soldiers ventured into this new-old no man's land.

During my free time back in blocking, when I wasn't playing cards or pitching horseshoes with my buddies, I often went to the target range to practice with the forty-five I'd been issued as a gunner. Now, I was good with a forty-five; that's no brag, just fact.

When I finished the company standard, our commander came to me and said, "Nick, your score with a forty-five qualifies you to continue on to battalion."

My score in the battalion competition qualified me for regiment. There, I got wiped out by a bunch of officers who could probably hit a target in their sleep. But I did make into the second grouping.

But the loud ringing in my ears hadn't gotten any better. If anything, it bothered me more. Maybe because life had become Army-normal again. I no longer had the distraction of combat. Nights were the worst time, lying in my cot, listening to that siren sound. It was about to drive me crazy.

So crazy that I considered going on sick call. Which was something I didn't want to do. First because it seemed such a minor thing, one I should be able to cope with, and I didn't want my buddies to think I wasn't tough enough to handle something so small. And second, because fear had set in.

Fear that something might happen to me now that it looked like the war was really over. It was one thing to get killed in combat, but I was scared of getting killed in some freak accident like those two guys on Outpost Tom who had been blown up in that chink hole, or the sergeant who was killed by a defective weapon, or my uncle in Denmark who made it all the way through World War II, then died when his ship hit a mine.

I knew the Army would keep me in Korea for awhile, but the fighting seemed to be over. I wasn't on death row anymore. Now, I desperately wanted to stay alive long enough to go home.

But it had gotten to the point where I couldn't stand this ringing in my ears one more minute. I convinced myself that, since it was such a small problem, there might be something the Army doctors could do to stop it. So I went on sick call.

They took me to the battalion medic. He asked what my problem was. I told him, "I've got this real bad ringing in my right ear. And when somebody hollers at me, I have trouble figuring out where the voice is coming from — which direction."

He looked inside my ear and announced, "You've got a hole in your eardrum. We'll send you back to Seoul to the psychiatrist."

A psychiatrist — I didn't know what good a psychiatrist could do for me. But I thought, what the hell.

"Okay," I said.

From battalion, I was taken to a depot and put on a Red Cross train. One of the volunteers came around passing out cigarettes and chocolate bars. And it was real chocolate, not all whitish in color like the discs in our C-rations.

When I arrived in Seoul, I was transported to the Army hospital that handled all the Section 9 cases. One of the doctors took a look at me and asked what my problem was. I told him about the ringing in my ears and my difficulty determining the direction of other sounds.

The psychiatrist frowned at that. "What are you doing here?"

I shrugged my shoulders. "I don't know. I went on sick call, told the doctor the same thing I told you, and he sent me here to a mental hospital."

The psychiatrist shook his head in disgust. "I'm going to assign you to a medical hospital. There's nothing we can do for you here."

So, off I went to a medical hospital. I figured the medic back at battalion thought I was suffering from battle fatigue. I probably never argued with him because I thought he might be right. I knew what I'd been during those first few days after Pendleton had died. From what I'd heard others say about battle fatigue, it sounded like that's what I had had back then.

At the regular hospital, I went through the whole question and answer procedure again. After I had explained my problem, they washed out my ears. It improved the hearing in my left ear, but it didn't help the ringing in my right ear at all.

Then I was informed that they were going to assign me to an outfit in Seoul. "But I don't know anybody in Seoul," I said, scared at the thought of being separated from my buddies. "Why can't I go back to my outfit. I know those guys. We've fought together."

"That should be all right," they told me. "We'll just have you put on light duty."

They also told me that they wanted me to come back two months before I was scheduled to rotate home. I didn't like the sound of that, even though that was over a year away. It was all tied up with that fear something would happen to keep me from going home. And if the doctors found something two months before I shipped out, they could easily mess around and keep me in Korea longer. I made up my mind right then that the only way they would ever see me again would be at the point of a gun; I wouldn't voluntarily go back.

Now that I was no longer considered one of the walking wounded, my trip back to my outfit didn't include a cushy train ride. Instead, I was loaded onto a deuce-and-a-half taken to the REPL depot, loaded into another truck and driven back to my battalion headquarters.

When I reported in, the sergeant looked at my papers and said, "You're on light duty.

"What does that mean?" I asked.

He smiled. "It means you don't have to do diddly-shit Just stay in your tent. If you want to clean the latrine now and then, that's fine."

I've worked all my life. I soon grew bored with doing nothing. So I went to the first sergeant, a World War II veteran and former glider pilot, and asked if there was an opening in the motor pool so I could at least drive a Jeep.

"I'll get you in there," he promised.

Bingo, I became the first sergeant's Jeep driver. At the time I had no idea that when you're assigned to light duty, you can just about name any job you want.

I spent a few months driving the first sergeant around, washing the Jeep and changing the oil. Now and then, we'd head up into the mountains and hunt pheasants or the small Korean deer.

After a while that got old. A guy who worked in the company kitchen came to me one day and said, "If you want an easy job and good food, Nick, you should put in for mine. All you have to do is go in early every morning and light the stoves. I'm rotating home and they're looking for somebody to take my place."

So I took over his job. This is one time when the Army food was good. One of the guys in our Dog Company had been a professional baker before the Army drafted him. He had taught the guys in the kitchen the art of making bread and pastries. It was a source of pride with us that our company commander often invited other officers over to sample the rolls and desserts from our kitchen.

Needless to say, I got first crack at all of it — and gained weight as a result. Working on the line also gave me a chance to make sure my buddies received extra helpings of the good stuff.

During those months following the cease-fire, when I was no longer under combat pressure, it became a common occurrence for me to wake up at night in a cold sweat, my skin crawling with the sensation of those body parts all over me. The vividness of it shook me. I couldn't take a shower to get rid of it, but I would wash face. Then I would sit up for an hour or two, smoking cigarettes and waiting for the memories to fade.

I never mentioned the nightmares to anyone. Blackburn was the only one who would have understood what I was going through, and he was a sergeant now in another platoon.

The others, especially the ones who had never been in combat, would probably have wondered why it still bothered me. I wondered the same thing myself. To me, it was like a sign of weakness. And I had that Fifties male mind-set that such things should be kept to yourself; a real man handled his own problems.

In a way, it was no different than the constant ringing in my ears. Don't complain, and don't give the Army a chance to keep you longer than your term of enlistment.

Maybe, after Seoul, if I had reported regularly for sick call with my hearing problems, the Army might have given me a medical discharge. I guess I'll never know.

When the time came for me to go back to the hospital in Seoul for a checkup, that was one appointment I was determined not to keep. When no one brought up the subject, I definitely didn't want to remind anyone about it.

Anyhow, I was too afraid something would happen to keep me from going home. And that fear increased as the time drew closer to rotate back to the States. It only got worse when my parents wrote in one of their letters that my friend Warren Krogan had died from cancer. First the guy had lost his leg to cancer; now it had taken his life.

Wild thoughts sprang into my mine — what if the truck I'm on hits a land mine? What if the Chinese launch an air strike? I must have come up with a hundred freak scenarios. But then, I had known guys who had been killed in freak accidents.

Finally I promised God that, if He made sure I got safely home, I would never complain about Council Bluffs, or Iowa, the United States or anything else ever again.

* * *

In September of 1954, my orders came through. The Army was shipping me home. I worried the whole way. On board the transport ship, I kept thinking — what if it sinks? Lord, you wouldn't let anything happen to me know, would you? Not after seeing me through the hell of combat?

It was almost worse when I actually saw the coastline. 'Dear God, please don't let another ship run into us.'

All that sounds crazy now, almost laughable. But at the time, the fear was real.

Needless to say, our ship docked without incident. By now, it had been a year and two-plus months since the cease-fire had taken effect. In the eyes of the public, the Korean War had been over for a long time.

Of course, it was never officially declared a war, only a police action. But if something looks like war, sounds like war, smells like war, feels like war, and has the same tinny taste of fear that war has, — it's war.

And I was just coming home from it. But there were no cheering crowds on the pier to welcome us, just an Army band and volunteers from the Red Cross passing out coffee and donuts. To be honest, that hurt. I had gone through hell in Korea, and I wanted somebody to care.

But I was back in the States, although I wasn't home yet. The next leg of my journey would take me to Fort Carson Colorado, on a twin-engine prop job. The turbulence over the Rocky Mountains was enough to make a sailor sick. I know I turned a couple shades of green and prayed fervently that the plane wouldn't crash.

After arriving safely at Fort Carson one of the first things I did was head for the PX and buy myself a quart of milk, a ring of bologna, and a bottle of genuine American beer, not that Korean saki stuff I'd had to drink over there.

While I was eating and drinking my purchases, one of the guys said, "Isn't that going to make you sick?"

"If it does, it'll be the happiest sick I've ever been," I told him. "In Korea, we never had ring bologna, American beer, or real milk, only the powdered kind you mix with water."

It's funny the things you miss when you're overseas.

I went through my final processing at Fort Carson and received my early discharge from the Army after roughly twenty-two months of service.

The separation document summed up my time in the Army in with simple military language. Under citations, I received the Korean Service Medal with one Bronze Service Star, Combat Infantry Badge (which meant I'd spent a minimum of thirty days under enemy fire), United Nations Service Medal, National Defense Service Medal, ROK Presidential Unit Citation, and Good Conduct Medal.

Other than the burns to my face and the damage to my hearing, I had come through the fighting without a scratch, so there was no Purple Heart. Nor was there any medal for my part in the firefight that had claimed Pendleton's life, one that the sergeant had said he would recommend for me. I never cared for myself, but it bothered me that I had never heard whether Pendleton had been awarded a medal. If anybody deserved one, he did.

From Fort Carson, I took the train home to Omaha. On the way, I went to the dining car and ordered myself a big steak.

The waiter, a black guy, looked at me, sitting there in my Army fatigues and warned, "It will be expensive."

"I've spent the last nineteen and a half months in Korea, and I want the biggest steak you've got even if I have to do dishes to pay for it."

He smiled and said, "One steak coming up."

He brought me a steak, so enormous it almost filled the plate. But I ate every bit of it. When he brought me the bill, it was only four dollars and some cents — this at a time when a steak dinner should have ten or fifteen dollars on a train.

"Wait a minute," I said. "There must be a mistake."

"Didn't you learn to keep your mouth shut in-the Army?" he challenged.

I got the message, loud and clear. "Yes, sir," I said and paid for my four dollar steak.

Ten

When I got off the train in Omaha, I caught a cab and went home. Naturally my family was glad to see me, but few of my friends seemed to remember that I'd even been gone, let alone that I'd been in Korea.

Basically I never talked about the fighting I'd seen, except in the most general terms, not even to my family. While I was in Korea, I never wrote home about the action I'd been in, not even after the fact, because I didn't want my folks to worry.

About the only thing I did admit to any of them was that my hearing problems were the result of a machine gun firing only inches from my ear. I don't recall any of my family questioning how that came to be.

As for my friends, they weren't really interested in what I'd been through. To them, it was old news. And I knew they wouldn't understand even if I told them. I'd learned that much in Korea. In a way, their indifference hurt; it made me think that I had wasted my time over there because nobody cared.

Every now and then, I would run into somebody who had been in Korea. A couple of them bragged about the firefights they'd been in. Yet, I knew for a fact they hadn't seen any action. It turned my stomach. If anything, it made me even less inclined to talk about my time in Korea.

It was something I wanted to forget about anyway. It wasn't easy, though. Still, I thought the memories would be like the ringing in my ears, the nightmares about Outpost Tom, and the severe headaches I had started having — headaches that were so bad that sometimes I literally pulled my hair out. I was sure that in time they would all go away.

Shortly after I got back, I went to see Warren Krogan's mother to offer my condolences over his death. While we were talking, she said something that I didn't quite catch. I apologized, explained that I had some hearing problems, and asked her to repeat it.

She jumped on that right away. "What do you mean, you're having hearing problems? There was never anything wrong with your hearing before. When did this start?"

I admitted that it had begun in Korea when a machine gun had been fired right beside my ear, but I didn't tell her anymore than that.

Right away, she insisted that I go to the VA hospital in Omaha and have a doctor check it out. I said I would, but I think she knew I was only saying that to satisfy her, and that I wouldn't bother to go, because she immediately said that she would make the appointment and go with me. There wasn't any way I could wiggle out of it.

Something like a week or two later, she went with me to the VA hospital. When I saw the doctor, I explained about my hearing problems and the severe headaches I'd been having.

My headaches, the doctor attributed to a delayed reaction to the stress of combat. He said that wasn't at all uncommon, and prescribed some mediation.

Then he tested my hearing. It turned out that I was completely deaf in my right ear and I had suffered a forty per cent loss in my left ear as well. He said he would file a disability claim for me. That sounded fine to me. But he never did explain why I heard this loud, high-pitched ringing in an ear that was supposed to be deaf.

By this time I had already went to work at Meadow Gold Dairy in Council Bluffs. I worked hard all day long, partied hard half the night, and went to bed too tired to dream. The occasions became increasingly less frequent when I would wake up in a cold sweat, my skin crawling with the feeling of pieces of skin all over it. And the pills the doctor prescribed for my headaches pretty well handled the pain.

I was doing fine until spring rolled around and along came one of those old-fashioned Midwest thunderstorms. With the first flash of lightning and boom of thunder, I dived under the nearest table, forgetting for a split second that I was in Iowa and thinking instead that I was back in Korea under an artillery barrage. I felt pretty danged foolish when I had to crawl out of my hidey-hole.

To this day, my muscles still tense up ready to spring for cover when I hear a really loud clap of thunder.

It's the same with a Fourth of July fireworks display. Everything about it reminds me of Korea. To me, the bright color-bursts look like flares lighting up the night sky; the BOOM of Roman candles are like exploding artillery shells; the whoosh of one launching and the spiraling whine of one falling sound like outgoing mail. And there's the same acrid smell of cordite and layer of smoke hanging in the air. I go to them because my family enjoys them, but I don't. Maybe I never will.

One Sunday afternoon in the summer of 1955, I didn't have much to do, so I decided to visit Jim Briddes, one of the guys who worked with me at Meadow Gold. I dropped by his house and found both Jim and his wife Joan at home, but they already had company — a very pretty blond. Jim introduced me to her, identifying her as Juanita, his wife's sister.

I swear it was love at first sight. After only a few dates, I knew I wanted to marry her, but she was reluctant. Finally Juanita said she would marry me if I would agree to give up drinking.

In the past, there had been some problems with alcohol in her family, and she didn't want live with any more of it.

I said, "Sure, I'll give up drinking."

It didn't sound like any big deal to me. After all, I wasn't a hard drinker; I just had a few beers when I was out with my buddies. Quitting would be easy to do, I thought.

Three months later, we ran off to Missouri and eloped. I quit drinking — and went through hell for six months. That's when I realized just how close I had come to being an alcoholic.

Not long after Juanita and I were married, I ran into my cousin Bud Fernside who was a commander at the Disabled American Veterans association. In passing, I mentioned that one of the doctors over at the VA had said he would file a disability claim for me on my hearing loss, and that I'd never heard anything more.

Bud suggested that I see if the DAV could help me learn the status of my claim.

I thought about it and agreed. With a wife to support, any extra money would come in handy.

With the help of the DAV I filed another claim with the government. When I had to go to Des Moines for a hearing to see if I was entitled to any benefits, a representative from the DAV went with me.

At the hearing, I learned that my claim had been rejected because my Army medical records indicated that my hearing loss had been caused by artillery explosions, which meant it wasn't considered to be service-oriented.

I explained that my hearing wasn't damaged by artillery, that it had been a combination of machine gun fire and grenade explosions. Since that wasn't what my records indicated, the government informed me that I would have to prove the damage was from machine gun fire and grenades, not artillery.

Luckily I had Klang's address. Since he was with me that night in the trench, I knew he could verify that my hearing loss had been the result of the machine gun fire and grenade explosions during that firefight. I wrote and asked him to send me a letter, confirming my story. Within a couple weeks, I received Klang's letter, backing up what I'd said.

We made another trip to Des Moines, this time with the letter. Now the guy from the government brought up the fact that I already had a hole in my eardrum prior to service.

At that moment, I was positive it was all over; that my existing hole provided the government with the perfect excuse to deny my claim. I was ready to throw in the towel and walk out.

But my DAV representative said, "Yes, he had a hole in his right eardrum prior to service. You knew it when you drafted him and accepted him anyway. You increased the damage he had. Now, he no longer has the hearing ability that he had when he went into the Army. You are responsible for that."

By the time it was all over, the government agreed that my hearing loss was service-related and that I was entitled to ten per cent disability.

My monthly check wasn't much, but every little bit helps when you're married.

As the years went by, things got better. Juanita and I were blessed with two beautiful children, a son, Nickolas Dick, III, and a daughter, Catherine. I stopped having the severe headaches after about five years. And the vivid nightmares of Outpost Tom became fairly rare.

Every now and then I would be notified about a coming reunion of the regiment, or individual groups within it like the 'Survivors of Outpost Harry', but I never went to any of them. And I never joined the VFW or any veterans group, or kept in touch with any of my Army buddies.

Korea was a part of my life I wanted to forget.

At the same time, I kept all the documents relating to my years in service, the photos I had taken over there, the sketchy diary I kept in Korea, and a book that covered the history of the Fifteenth Regiment in Korea. But I never looked at any of them.

Then in 1987, I was hurt on the job at Meadow Gold Dairy. As a result of the injury, I had to have back and neck surgery. For weeks after the operation, I wasn't allowed to do anything.

For a man who had worked all his life, always been physically active, to suddenly be forced to do nothing, was hard. I sat around all day long watching television or movies rented from the video store.

I was tied to the house, but I didn't feel that Juanita should be, too. So I asked our neighbor to take her out to breakfast once in awhile.

During those times when I was alone in the house, I started having re-occurrences of combat. I'd be sitting in my living room, but in my mind, I was in Korea, seeing those pale, hunched over shapes jumping the trench, hearing Pendleton holler "Chinese!" and the machine hammering beside my ear. I'd yell or blurt out things, anything to try to get rid of the images that were alive in my mind.

And the dreams began again. It got to where I didn't want to go to bed, because I knew some time during the night, I would wake up in a cold sweat, back on Outpost Tom, staring at those bits of skin with hair growing out of them that were on my arm. Each time it happened, I'd get up, take a shower, and try to scrub away the sensation.

At the same time, while I was recuperating from the surgery, our little dog Angel died very suddenly at the age of eight from an aneurysm. I was already depressed, but losing Angel, my daily companion, got me down even more.

But I never told anybody what I was going through, not my grown children or Juanita. I had promised God I wouldn't complain about anything, and I was determined to keep that promise.

I have always been a happy, easy-going guy, quick to crack jokes and laugh. That began to change after my surgery and the re-occurrences started. Anytime Juanita mentioned how quiet I was, or how quick I was to snap at her, I always blamed it on boredom or the pain I was having.

While it was true that I was bored and in pain, that wasn't the reason for the change in my personality. Deep down, I think I knew that.

But I kept telling myself that once I recovered and got back on my feet, this Korea stuff would go away. In the meantime, I just needed to be man enough to tough it out and keep my mouth shut.

When the day finally came when I was required to walk so many miles a day as part of my therapy, it seemed to help. At least walking kept me from having so much free time to think and remember.

But the job injury and resulting surgery marked the end of my working career. According to the doctors, I didn't have any choice but to reach a settlement on my workman's compensation claim with my employer and take an early retirement.

In 1988, I officially joined the ranks of the retired. But I knew that if I wanted to get Korea off my mind, I had to do something to keep myself occupied. Since my wife and I had done a lot of weekend camping over the years, we decided to trade in our small camper for a motor home and do more traveling.

Keep moving. Don't stay still. Just go, go, go. I thought that would be the answer, but it wasn't.

Just about everywhere we went during the next few years, I saw something that reminded me of Korea. The mountains of Kentucky were the worst because they looked so much like the rugged hills in Korea.

Time after time while I was driving through Kentucky, I would spot a section of terrain that reminded me of the area around Outpost Harry or the hill we called Five Fingers, and I would focus in on it. Suddenly I'd start seeing the hunched-over figures of Chinese soldiers in their mustard-colored caps scrambling up the slopes. Just like that I would be back in Korea, not driving down a Kentucky highway.

I don't know how many times Juanita hit me and said, "Nick, you're driving off the road. What is the matter with you?"

At first, I made some excuse, claimed I had dozed off or something. Later I started snapping back at her, swearing because she'd hit me.

You have to understand that, in all our previous married life, I rarely ever used profanity around her. Now it laced my language almost all the time — the same as it had in Korea.

Every day I seemed to get a little meaner. Not physically, but verbally. Suddenly Juanita and I were arguing constantly over something. And that wasn't like me.

I have never been the type of person to quarrel over anything. I would rather walk away, even if it meant letting the other person think he was right. Now, here I was, picking fights with my wife.

And the nightmares were always with me. At first I sloughed off Juanita's questions when she asked why I had taken a shower in the middle of the night, by saying I felt dirty.

Then one fateful night, I was sitting at our kitchen table, my hair still wet from the shower when Juanita came out of our bedroom and saw me.

"Did you take a shower, Nick?"

"As a matter of fact, I did. What of it?"

"But why would you take a shower? You haven't done anything to get dirty

"So what?"

"So — why did you take one?"

After years of saying nothing, this time I blurted out, "I had these pieces of skin all over me. I had to get them off."

"Pieces of skin?"

"Yeah. From Korea." By then I realized what I'd done. Suddenly there was no turning back.

"From Korea? What are you talking about, Nick?"

She was looking at me like I was crazy. Sometimes I thought I was. So I told her a very censored version of what had happened on Outpost Tom.

When I finished, she said, "Nick, you need to see a doctor. You need help."

"No, I'll be fine," I insisted. "I can handle this."

"No, you can't. Nick, you have turned a stranger. There's something wrong with you. You're not yourself any more. You need help."

"Dammit, I said I'd be fine."

Thank God, she didn't believe me and gave me an ultimatum instead. "Either you get help, Nick, or I am getting a divorce."

At this point, you have to understand something about me. I have never believed in going to psychiatrists or the like, even though our daughter Cathie is a counselor. I have always felt that a man should solve his own problems, and that there was something lacking in him if he sought help from a psychiatrist.

But my wife was threatening to leave me after forty-odd years of marriage. Juanita doesn't make idle threats. If I didn't do something, she would leave.

So, I contacted the veterans group in Pottawatamie County. They put me in touch with a court officer, filed a claim for me and gave me the name of a counselor in Omaha. Reluctantly, I made an appointment with him to appease my wife.

On my first visit, I told him about the problems I'd been having — that even though the Korean War had ended nearly fifty years ago, I still remembered it as if it were yesterday. Images from combat plagued my mind night and day. Any time I closed my eyes, I saw the blood and wetness from the body parts that landed on me when I was lying in the trench. I could still smell the putrid stench of corpses rotting in the field, unable to be retrieved. I can hear guys crying for help, and there's nothing I can do for them. I can still feel Pendleton pushing at me, yelling for me and Klang to leave. I can still the smoke and dust from the explosion that took his life.

I asked the counselor why I remembered everything about Korea so vividly — the sights, the sounds, the smell, the terrain — when others didn't?

He explained that I was describing something that was known as Posttraumatic Stress Disorder, experienced by people who had been through some traumatic event, whether it be combat, rape, serious accidents, or such natural disasters as earthquakes, fires or floods. At some point after the event, victims began to have re-occurring nightmares and daytime fantasies that can be triggered by something as simple as a knock on a door or the particular shape of a hill. He also told me that medical science didn't fully understand why some people suffered from it while others didn't even though they had experienced the same thing.

He also told me it wasn't at all uncommon that the problem hadn't surfaced until after I retired. My mind wasn't occupied anymore with the demands of work. Now it had lots of free time to think and remember.

According to him, I had kept the horror of my experience inside for too long. I needed to talk about it — not just gloss over it with simple fact, but tell all of it — what I saw, what I heard, what I felt, what I thought. He also said that my family needed to hear my story, and suggested that my wife and daughter come with me on my next appointment. In the meantime, he made arrangements for me to see a psychiatrist at the VA Hospital in Omaha so I could have some medication prescribed

Juanita and Cathie went with me on my next visit to the counselor. I gave them the basic details of the things that had happened to me in Korea, but I still held a lot of things back. I don't know whether I did it to protect them or me.

I do know that I've told you stuff I never even mentioned to the counselor. Some of it, I think I had blocked out. I didn't want to remember, but you made me.

For eight, long months, I made regular visits to the counselor. At first, I went twice a week. But that seemed to make things worse. It was like being in Korea every single day. So I ended up going to him just once a week.

It wasn't easy, let me tell you. Every time I had to go, I got scared because I knew the minute I stepped into his office, I would be back in Korea.

To make things worse, he didn't know anything about the history of the Korean War. The first time I said something about the Chinese attacking us, he questioned me, wanting to know why I referred to the North Koreans as Chinese. The man actually didn't know that Communist China had sent their armies to fight with the North Koreans.

Another time, he asked me how long it was after the cease-fire before peace was declared. There was never any declaration of peace, only a cease-fire. How can there be a declaration of peace when there was never a declaration of war?

You can bet he knew all about Vietnam and World War II, but he didn't know beans about Korea. At times, it got pretty damned frustrating, too.

Almost nothings has been written about the fighting during the latter months of the war before the cease-fire. Most of the books about the Korean War focus on the initial invasion by the North Koreans, MacArthur landing his troops at Inch'on Harbor and taking the offensive, driving the North Koreans back across the Thirty-Eight parallel, and the Chinese forces subsequently joining in to drive MacArthur's troops back across the line. Even the history books dwell mostly on the on-going peace talks in 1953, relegating the fighting to a few pages — and in some cases, only a few paragraphs.

I've been told it's because there were no big battles involving thousands of troops during those last months of the war. That is true. But some of the bloodiest fighting happened during that period just the same. Even the historians admit that.

But it barely rates a paragraph in most history books.

I read somewhere that two million people were killed during the Korean War; roughly forty thousand of those were Americans. But most people today don't know that; what's more they don't care.

I guess that's why sometimes I feel like it was all a big waste of my time.

The counselor asked me once if I felt bitter. I don't. Even though every night when I lay down, I have Korea roaring in my ears, I have always considered myself to be one of the lucky ones. I came home. Maybe I did lose most of my hearing over there. But too many others lost their lives. Guys who were buddies of mine. Guys like Pendleton. Other than their families, nobody knows about the ultimate sacrifice they made. And it still bothered me that, as far as I knew, Pendleton had never received a medal.

That doesn't make me bitter or angry. It makes me sad.

The counselor's ignorance accomplished one thing, though: it made me dig out my photographs from Korea, the regimental history book, the crude diary I kept, and various documents and papers. After years of avoiding contact with other Korean veterans, I started attending the odd meeting or reunion. I also tried tracking down some of the guys in my outfit through the Internet, with the help of my daughter Cathie.

About two years ago, she called me up one day and said, "Dad, what was the name of that corporal on the machine gun, the one you recommended for a medal?"

"Pendleton. Why?"

"Charles F. Pendleton, Company D 15th Infantry Regiment?"

"I don't remember whether his first name was Charles or not, but that's our outfit. What about him?" I asked.

"You don't have to worry anymore about whether he was awarded a medal. He got one, Dad, — the biggest one of all. Corporal Charles F. Pendleton received the Congressional Medal of Honor."

I wept when she told me that. And I wasn't ashamed of my tears.

All these years I thought that he had never received any kind of medal, that he had saved so many lives and not even the Army had recognized him for it. I felt like I had let him down somehow. Instead, Pendleton had been posthumously awarded the Congressional Medal of Honor.

Later I heard that his family had the medal on display in some school in Texas. I'm still trying to find out where in Texas. Some day I'd like to go there and see it for myself. But at least, he knows I kept the promise I made to him that night in the trench.

It's funny how much better I feel about things now. You can call Korea the Forgotten War if you want to, but I haven't forgotten it. I probably never will. And you know what? That's all right. Because if I forget it, then it would mean forgetting the men who served beside me — the ones who came home and the ones who didn't. And I don't want to forget either.

I'm proud of them, and I'm proud of my country. To this day, I still get a lump in my throat when I see the American flag coming down the street in a parade. That sounds corny, doesn't it? But I've learned that the things you feel deeply about always sound corny when you have to put them into words.

That's just the way it is.

And that's just the way it was for me in Korea.

Biography

Nicholas Dick Jr.

Nicholas Dick Jr. saw grueling combat action during the Korean War. This is his gripping autobiography told as only a soldier can tell it-- from the foxhole. Despite his injuries, he survived to produce this provactive tale of men at war.

Biography

Janet Dailey

Janet Dailey was born Janet Haradon in 1944 in Storm Lake, Iowa. She attended secretarial school in Omaha, Nebraska before meeting her husband, Bill. Bill and Janet worked together in construction and land development until they "retired" to travel throughout the United States, inspiring Janet to write the Americana series of romances, where she set a novel in every state of the Union. In 1974, Janet Dailey was the first American author to write for Harlequin. Her first novel was NO QUARTER ASKED. She has since gone on to write approximately 90 novels, 21 of which have been on the New York Times Bestseller List. She has won many awards and accolades for her work, appearing widely on radio and television. Today, there are over three hundered million Janet Dailey books in print, in 19 different languages, making her one of the most popular novelists in the world.

Printed in the United States
1546500001B/233-236